THE NEW
ETIQUETTE
GUIDE TO
GETTING
MARRIED
AGAIN

OTHER BOOKS BY THE AUTHOR

BY MARJABELLE YOUNG STEWART AND ANN BUCHWALD
White Gloves and Party Manners
Stand Up, Shake Hands, Say "How Do You Do?"
What to Do When...and Why

BY MARJABELLE YOUNG STEWART AND MARIAN FAUX
Executive Etiquette

BY MARJABELLE YOUNG STEWART
Your Complete Wedding Planner
Looking Pretty, Feeling Fine

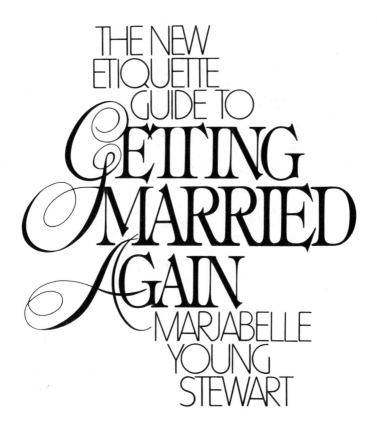

THE NEW ETIQUETTE GUIDE TO GETTING MARRIED AGAIN

MARJABELLE YOUNG STEWART

ST. MARTIN'S PRESS • NEW YORK

Library of Congress Cataloging in Publication Data

Stewart, Marjabelle Young.
The new etiquette guide to getting married again.

Includes index.
1. Wedding etiquette. 2. Remarriage. I. Title.
BJ2065.R44S83   395'.22   79-23004
ISBN 0-312-56749-9

To my beloved husband, Bill, and my dear son, Billy, who fill my life with love, happiness, and fulfillment.

ACKNOWLEDGMENTS

My special thanks to Marian Faux for applying to the manuscript her literary skills and outstanding talent; my gratitude to my editor, Barbara Anderson, for her encouragement, patience, and professional know-how, all of which made this book possible.

CONTENTS

PREFACE

*M*arriage must have something to recommend it, since more and more persons are getting married than ever before—and many are giving marriage a try for the second or third time. Getting married again, however, is not like the first time around. For one thing, it poses a new set of personal relationships to be established—with your ex-husband and in-laws, with your new husband's children and family, even, in many instances, with your own friends. Then, too, you ask yourself lots of questions that you somehow didn't ask the first time around. How do you tell your children you are going to get married? Can they participate in the ceremony? Can you wear white? A veil? Carry a traditional bridal bouquet? Do persons give you gifts this time? For that matter, can you have a large, tradition-filled wedding and reception? In short, how much celebrating is within the boundaries of good taste?

The answer is that as much celebrating as you want is acceptable, although there are ways of remarrying that reflect tact and good taste. This book is your guide to planning an *appropriate* second wedding that satisfies all your desires and longings and fantasies.

There has probably never been a better time to get married, particularly if you are not marrying for the first time. In the fifties, etiquette was stiff and formal, and a lot of tradition and ceremony was denied to a woman who had been married before. Wedding etiquette, in some instances, seemed designed more to penalize a woman for having been married before than to celebrate the beginning of her new union. Frankly, the list of don'ts was a mile long. In the sixties, etiquette was largely nonexistent, particularly among those who were marrying, and so were the ceremonies and traditions that make a wedding memorable.

The seventies have seen a return to a sense of balance and the rise of the New Etiquette, a code of behavior that stresses feelings rather than rules. The old, rigid rules are gone—forever, one hopes—and an affection for tradition and ceremony has returned. After all, getting married is and should be a joyous occasion. It is an occasion for celebration, whatever your previous marital status and whatever your age.

I have written this book primarily as a sourcebook, a collection of ideas garnered from my own second wedding and from the experiences of countless others who have remarried. All kinds of weddings and receptions and, for that matter, lifestyles, are described in these pages. The reader has only to choose from among the numerous suggestions and ideas those that will combine to make her wedding day special and unique.

While a book on remarrying is mainly concerned with the planning of the wedding and reception, persons who are remarrying often have other things to consider: stepparenting, new relationships with inlaws, merging two households or beginning a new one, merging two careers, making decisions about financial arrangements, and in some cases, drawing up marriage contracts. All these subjects are dealt with in this book, along with numerous ideas and hints on how to plan the wedding and reception.

Getting married again is *not* like getting married for the first time. This is the first book to recognize that fact and to discuss the differences between this wedding and your first wedding, in addition to how to handle this one graciously and smoothly.

Good luck in your new life.

Marjabelle Young Stewart

Chapter One

PLANNING
YOUR WEDDING

S *o* you have decided to take the big step and get married again. And somewhere in the midst of all that glow and the good feelings and love that you are feeling right now, you may be nursing a few apprehensions about how to plan this wedding. After all, you *have* been married before, and aren't there a lot of rules about what you can and cannot do if you have been married before? And what about all the intricate relationships—his kids, your kids, your ex-inlaws, his ex-inlaws, your parents, his parents? Sorting out your feelings about these relationships and blending them with a wedding and reception that will not leave behind a string of hurt feelings isn't easy.

You also have to realize that you are different, too, from that woman who walked down the aisle the first time. You are older and, presumably, you bring a different set of emotions to this marriage than you brought to the first. They may affect the kind of ceremony you want this time.

Then, too, few persons have the slightest desire to duplicate their first wedding. More likely, you will want to avoid any similarities. If you walked down the aisle in a formal wedding dress with a train and ten-foot-long veil, and were preceded by five attendants, you will probably want a quieter wedding ceremony this time. On the other hand, if you were married in a civil ceremony with two strangers as witnesses, you may want to make up for what you did not have. Don't worry—you certainly can do just that.

While etiquette has lost much of its stiffness on the issue of remarriage, there are a few guidelines of good taste to which you will probably want to adhere. The old rules about remarrying have mostly fallen by the wayside, but this book will show you how to plan a second wedding that is the wedding of your dreams, in addition to being tasteful and considerate of everyone's feelings.

Perhaps the most enjoyable aspect of this wedding is that it is truly yours. You alone—or you and your future husband—plan this wedding. Your parents may or may not offer financial assistance, but they will rarely play so decisive a role as they did in your first wedding.

Since you can have the kind of wedding you dream of, and since you will have control of the planning, then what are the guidelines? How do you marry again in good taste?

WHAT THE RULEBOOKS SAY

Most etiquette books state that if the groom has been married before, this officially has no bearing on the size and shape of this wedding. This rule is based on the theory that every woman is entitled to have an innocent, formal, large wedding at least once. (In reality, the groom may have definite feelings on this subject, either in terms of making up for what he did not do the first time or in terms of avoiding a large, fancy wedding, so it is only tactful to discuss this with him before making any arrangements.)

A woman who is divorced and remarrying traditionally does not have a large, ultraformal wedding, although she can have a large wedding, formal or informal (see chapter 3 on dress). She doesn't wear a bridal veil, is not given in marriage by her father or anyone else and, in short, does not plan her wedding in any way that appears to deny that she was married before. This is not to say that this wedding cannot be a dressy, romantic, sophisticated event—or whatever you like—it just should not fittingly be as "bridish" as your first wedding was. This book contains many hints on having a lovely, special wedding *sans* bridish overtones.

A widow traditionally does not wear a white bride's dress, nor does she wear a veil. She does not do anything that ignores the fact that she, too, was married previously. She may, unlike a divorced woman, be given in marriage by a male relative, including a son old enough to handle the responsibility. Most widows, actually, have weddings much like those of divorced women— large, gay parties that are as dressy as they like but which avoid any notes or overtones generally reserved for a first wedding.

If you are catching on to the fact that the mood of your wedding is more important than any rules you choose to follow or break, then you are beginning to be comfortable with the idea of getting married again graciously.

WHEN ETIQUETTE AND YOUR
DESIRES CONFLICT

You may find that you truly want to do something—to wear a wedding dress, for example—that isn't exactly in accordance with the rulebook. How do you handle this? Since a wedding is a very special day, and since it is your day, if you find yourself in conflict with custom, you should probably go ahead and do whatever you want to do. There are few enough times in life when one gets another chance, and if you feel that you truly want to wear a wedding dress that looks young and innocent, even if you aren't, then go ahead. To alleviate any clucking, you or your mother—whose friends may be far more worried about this than any of your peers—might just pass the word that "A wedding dress has always been one of Susy's dreams, and she didn't wear one the first time, so she's going to this time." That way, your Great Aunt Minnie can be prepared for "the worst" in advance.

What matters is that you not create an aura of never having been married before. That would be hypocritical. On the other hand, satisfying your special desires and playing out a few of your fantasies is something you can do no matter how many times you've been married. In this book, we'll talk about the traditions and customs of weddings—the ones that normally are and are not followed when you have been married previously—but only you should make the final decision about what you want to do.

THE ENGAGEMENT—ALWAYS A HECTIC TIME

While this engagement will be different from your earlier one, in one way it will be exactly the same. No matter how small a wedding you plan, it will grow to some degree, and it will consume far more of your time than you ever imagined. So the best thing to do is to begin organizing the minute you know you are going to marry again. Even small weddings and receptions take time and planning if you want perfection—and most of us want this lovely day to be as special and romantic as possible, in every way.

ANNOUNCING YOUR WEDDING PLANS

Official public announcements, that is, newspaper announcements, are often not made for second marriages. The exception is when either the bride or groom is known professionally, and the news of the marriage is just that—news. In that case, a newspaper may print news of your plans without your asking them to. You may also announce your wedding plans officially, if you want to. Most newspapers will have forms for this purpose; they are supplied by the society editor.

Personal relationships will be more complicated to sort out when you make the announcement. Your children may have their own feelings about your impending marriage; your husband-to-be may also have children or family with whom this new personal relationship must be worked out. For that reason, you may want to delay any public announcement of your engagement until everyone involved has been informed of your plans and has had time to become comfortable with them.

Finally, because of the necessity of sorting out your

personal relationships during the engagement, many couples fail to take time for romantic evenings alone that would be natural for another couple without any special family entanglements. While merging two households and possibly one or more sets of kids does take precedence, remember to save some special evenings to be alone with each other, to anticipate the pleasures of your marriage and your new lives together.

PLANNING THE KIND AND SIZE
OF THE CEREMONY

Several factors determine the size and style of the wedding you will have this time. First, are your previous marriages. With each succeeding marriage, you will probably want to skip one or two of the small traditions. Generally, the kind of wedding and reception you plan will be smaller and more intimate.

Second, you must consider any religious restrictions. In fact, before making any plans for a religious ceremony, contact your clergyman. Tell him one or both of you have been previously married. Ask whether or not he will be willing to marry you again. If so, will he marry you in the rectory or the main sanctuary? He may suggest a chapel wedding. Explain if you want to wear a formal wedding dress or follow any other formal tradition. The clergyman may not be willing to perform anything other than a small, quiet ceremony. If so, you must either look for someone else to marry you or accept his restrictions.

The third and final determining factor is money. Weddings and receptions of any size are expensive. It would seem that cutting down on the number of guests would reduce these costs, but more often than not, you simply end up spending more per guest. Then, too, the bride's parents rarely pay for this wedding. And even if your parents offer to give you a wedding, wouldn't it be nicer to spend your own money and have the freedom to plan exactly the kind of event you want? It is also acceptable these days for the bride and groom to share expenses for a wedding when either or both have been married before. In fact, any woman who has been living on her own and who runs her own household may pay for all or part of her wedding. All these things must be considered when you decide what kind of wedding you will have.

You also need to decide what you can afford. Do you want a small, private ceremony and an equally small but special dinner in a good French restaurant later? If you want fifty friends to be present at the ceremony, you will probably want to splurge on an especially lovely dress for the church and put your money into floral decorations for the altar. Or would you prefer to be married quietly and then have a big party, complete with live music and lots of food? In this case, most of your money will go into the entertainment fund, and you will probably have no flowers or a single bouquet at the church and wear simple clothes, preferring instead to spend a lot on the dress you will wear at the reception. Before you plan your wedding, you must reach decisions about these money related matters.

Any wedding can be as private or as public as you want it to be. If you want to have only your children and your parents at the ceremony, your friends will not take offense. Neither should anyone bat an eye if you decide to invite a lot of persons to the wedding and have a fancy reception.

Generally, though, when getting married again, some kinds of ceremonies have gained more favor than others. You should pretty much rule out an ultraformal wedding, with lots of attendants and the accompanying show. Such a wedding looks too much as if you are ignoring the fact that you were married before.

The smallest private wedding you can plan is a civil one, where you go to city hall and are married quietly, with just the two of you present. But even if you want to be married this quietly, why not add a few festive notes? At a minimum, ask two close friends to go along as your witnesses and then the four of you can share a wedding lunch. Wear a new, pretty outfit and carry a nosegay.

Another kind of ceremony frequently chosen is the private church ceremony. But often this is followed by a large, glorious reception with all the traditional trimmings.

You can even have a formal ceremony, if that is your desire. You just have to tailor it so you don't give the impression that you are forgetting that you were married before. Skip the bevy of bridesmaids, but settle on one, or possibly even two, attendants. You can also wear the prettiest dress you can find, but it shouldn't look too bridish. That means, instead of looking innocent, you can look sophisticated or romantic. You can wear a white evening dress, if you like, but it is better not to choose a formal wedding dress.

Other possibilities for an elegant, sophisticated wedding are a ceremony in a judge's chambers, especially when the judge is a close friend; a garden wedding; a home wedding; or a wedding in a restaurant, private club, or some other public place. Also lovely is a rectory or chapel wedding.

Afternoon or evening is the most popular time to schedule a wedding these days. Fashionable afternoon weddings are scheduled for 4:00 or 4:30 P.M. but they can be held any time. An evening wedding is usually held at 8 P.M. In the South, weddings are frequently scheduled for 8 or 9 P.M. to avoid the heat.

ATTENDANTS

Lots of young, girlish attendants are not usually part of the getting-married-again scene. For one thing, your attendants are chosen from your close circle of friends, so presumably they will be your own age. You should ask a close friend to stand up for you, and the groom should choose a best man. If many persons are attending the ceremony, ushers may be necessary to seat the guests. You need one usher for every fifty to seventy-five guests.

Groomsmen dress identically to the groom if the wedding is formal—black tie or white tie. If dinner jackets are worn, attendants may wear their own, or if a more identical look is desired, they may all rent their outfits.

Female attendants may all dress alike, but when you have one attendant, a tactful bride often suggests that her honor attendant wear something she already owns or buy a dress that she can wear on other occasions rather than a traditional bridesmaid's dress. The bridesmaid and bride need not even shop together, although the bride may go along to suggest what she thinks will fit in with the style of her wedding. Since the bride often wears a colored or print dress, she should describe in detail what she plans to wear so that her attendants' outfits are coordinated with hers in terms of color and style.

An attendant is accorded all the honor at this wedding that she would be at any wedding. It is an honor to attend a friend at her wedding, but an attendant is also doing you a favor. Attendants should be given presents to thank them for their help, although delightfully, at this wedding, you can dispense with the more traditional gift ideas if you want and buy something either more elegant, such as a sterling pen or letter opener, or a more practical gift, such as something for an attendant's home. A case of wine is an appropriate and thoughtful gift.

As a rule, you won't want to ask someone to attend you at this wedding who was your attendant at an earlier wedding. If you have remained best friends with someone over the years, however, and that is the only person whom you would like standing beside you, be sure to discuss the person's feelings before asking for her services as your attendant. Generally, rather than ask a previous attendant to stand up for you again, one asks children or does not have any attendants.

YOUR CHILDREN AS ATTENDANTS

If you like, your children can stand up for you at your wedding. A female child up to the age of seven or eight could easily be a flower girl and a little boy of the same age might be a ring bearer. A teenaged or grown daughter might want to be your honor attendant; this is fine. Children older than seven or eight and not yet old enough to assume the responsibilities of honor attendant pose a slight problem, as there is no official role for them. I have attended several lovely weddings, however, where the children merely stood quietly beside their parent as she or he married again. They had no official role, but they felt very much a part of the ceremony.

First, determine by talking with your children what rule, if any, they will feel comfortable with. Remember that your children need not even be present at this wedding, and they certainly should not participate if they don't want to.

Children who do not stand up with you, but are present, should be given seats of honor in the first pew, or they should stand near the front of the guests if the wedding is in a judge's chambers or at home.

As a rule, persons who have been married before are not given away when they marry again. But a widow may be given in marriage by a son, if he is old enough to do this graciously, or by some other relative, if she chooses.

Male children who attend you should be dressed in keeping with the formality of the affair. If the groom wears black tie, they should, too. If dark suits are the order of the day, this is appropriate dress for male children.

A daughter who acts as her mother's honor attendant should also dress in keeping with the formality of the wedding, but she should not wear a dress that is obviously meant for a bridesmaid. She is much more appropriately dressed in a pretty, long dress that she might wear on any formal or dressy occasion.

PLANNING THE KIND OF RECEPTION

A reception for a wedding where one or both parties have previously been married can be as large and as lively or as small and as intimate an event as you like. Dinner for six in your favorite restaurant is perfectly acceptable.

A reception is most often paid for by the bride and groom. A divorced or widowed woman may either pay for her own wedding or share expenses with the groom. A wedding reception can also be given by a bride's parents, or, if they offer, by a relative, or a friend. Occasionally, a friend will offer an especially lovely home or garden for a wedding; this is not to be confused with offering to give (and pay for) the reception. You may feel free to accept such a kind invitation, but assume that you will be paying your own expenses.

APPROPRIATE TRADITIONS
FOR THE RECEPTION

You can do anything you like, but there are some ways to make the reception for this wedding unique. Have a white cake if you like, traditional to the small bride and groom sitting atop it, but also consider how lovely a pastel cake or a cake decorated with flowers instead of figures would be.

Any kind of music you choose is fine, but if you had a popular band at your first wedding, how about a more sedate string quartet or a violinist and a cellist at this one?

There is no formal receiving line for this wedding,

but you and your new husband should stand close by the door and greet your guests as they arrive at the reception. You may also decide to greet your guests at the back of the church. Your parents, children, and attendants do not receive guests with you at this wedding. Because you are given fewer presents at this wedding—technically, no one owes you another wedding gift who gave a first one—it is probably more tactful not to open any presents at the reception. If guests bring them, as is a growing custom these days, simply have a table set up inconspicuously to hold them and then arrange for someone to remove them after the reception to your new home. If persons have sent gifts ahead and you have opened them, the receiving line is the time and place to convey your thanks, although you must still write thank-you notes, too.

Many of the traditions associated with getting married are dispensed with this time around. These include throwing the bouquet, throwing your garter, and being showered with rice as you leave the church or reception—the rice is to bring fertility, anyway, so you may want to be especially careful to avoid this custom.

Fortunately, everyone is a lot less silly about this wedding, and you won't have to act the role of the blushing bride—or live in fear of being given a shivaree.

SHOWERS AND OTHER ENTERTAINMENTS

You do not have showers this time; that would be asking for gifts, and no one, as mentioned earlier, is obligated to give you a wedding present. But since many persons will want to give you a wedding present anyway, expecting shower gifts is excessive and should be avoided.

This hardly means, though, that a flurry of parties cannot surround this wedding. You can entertain your friends when you announce your plans to marry and, thereafter, you will probably receive many invitations to parties and dinners in your honor. Accept them all—and enjoy them all. One of the lovely things about this round of prewedding entertaining, unlike your first, is that you will usually be asked to attend activities together to avoid the appearance of a shower. It's more fun this way.

You need not have a luncheon or dinner for your attendants but, of course, a wedding is an excuse for a party. Rather than planning a traditional luncheon, you might simply arrange to treat your attendant to a special, lovely lunch at the time that the two of you shop for your outfits or for her outfit. Or you and your new husband might make it a point to invite the persons who stand up for you to be your first dinner guests after you are married. The dinner should be special and festive, with excellent food and fine wines. This is a good time, if you haven't done so earlier, to present your attendants with mementoes of your wedding—presents and pictures.

Since there is not usually a rehearsal for a small wedding, there may not be any reason for a rehearsal dinner. Bachelor dinners, too, are usually skipped this time.

ORGANIZING EVERYTHING

All weddings, however large or small, public or private, take time, energy, and money. The first chart helps you budget wedding and reception expenses. The second chart shows how to plan your time efficiently and get everything done with time left over to relax and enjoy yourselves.

WEDDING AND RECEPTION BUDGET

	Estimated Cost	Actual Cost
Stationery		
Invitations	$___	$___
Announcements	$___	$___
Notepaper for thank-you cards	$___	$___
Reception napkins	$___	$___
Matches	$___	$___
Other (maps, at-home cards)	$___	$___
Total	$___	$___
Flowers		
Wedding		
Ceremony site (church, hotel, etc.)	$___	$___
Bride's, attendants' bouquets	$___	$___
Corsages for mothers	$___	$___
Boutonnieres for groom, best man	$___	$___
Reception		
Buffet decorations	$___	$___
Table centerpieces	$___	$___
Cake table	$___	$___
Other (bandstand)	$___	$___
Total	$___	$___
Photography		
Wedding portraits		
Formal	$___	$___
Candids	$___	$___
Total	$___	$___

	Estimated Cost	Actual Cost
Catering		
Reception		
Food	$_____	$_____
Liquor	$_____	$_____
Waiters, bartenders, etc.	$_____	$_____
Wedding cake	$_____	$_____
Total	$_____	$_____
Music		
Wedding (organist, soloist)	$_____	$_____
Reception (orchestra, combo)	$_____	$_____
Total	$_____	$_____
Bride's Outfit		
Dress	$_____	$_____
Headpiece	$_____	$_____
Accessories	$_____	$_____
Total	$_____	$_____
New Clothes	$_____	$_____
Fees		
Church, hotel or party rental, etc.	$_____	$_____
Clergyman	$_____	$_____
Ceremony assistants (cantor,		
sexton, etc.)	$_____	$_____
Total	$_____	$_____
Gifts		
Attendants'	$_____	$_____
Groom's and bride's gifts to		
each other	$_____	$_____
Wedding rings	$_____	$_____
Total	$_____	$_____

	Estimated Cost	Actual Cost
Transportation		
Limousines	$___	$___
Parking	$___	$___
Total	$___	$___
Total Wedding Costs	$___	$___

WEDDING AND RECEPTION COUNTDOWN CHECKLIST

As soon as you decide to marry:
1. Meet with clergyman to see if he will marry you and to arrange for type of wedding you want.
2. Decide on the type of wedding and reception you want.
3. Draw up a guest list.
4. Get names of suppliers (ask friends, check Yellow Pages) and call them to get estimates for the kinds of services you need.

Three to Four Months before Wedding: *
1. Reserve the place for the reception if wedding is being held elsewhere than in a home. If held at home, reserve the rental equipment you will need: tables, chairs, etc.
2. Reserve the caterer.
3. Book the musicians.
4. Order invitations and any other stationery you need.
5. Meet with the florist.
6. Engage a photographer or ask a friend to take photos.
7. Order the wedding cake.
8. Ask close friends to attend you; line up anyone else whose help you will need on wedding day.
9. Shop for wedding dress. Discuss dress with honor attendant and possibly go with her to shop.

*Less time is needed to organize a small wedding than a large one or a home wedding rather than a reception in a club or hall.

Two Months before the Wedding:
1. Firm up final plans with caterer, florist, baker, and musicians.
2. Organize your clothes for your new life and shop for any new things you will need.
3. Talk about a wedding trip or vacation and begin to make firm plans. Apply for or renew your passport if necessary.
4. Discuss living arrangements and look for house or apartment if you will need to move.
5. Make any financial arrangements that are necessary: change or open bank accounts, change insurance policies, rewrite wills. Draw up any contracts about your possessions and living arrangements. Start changing credit cards and legal documents if you will change your name.
6. Shop for wedding bands and wedding gifts for each other.
7. Shop for any new household possessions you will need.

One Month before the Wedding:
1. Address and mail invitations.
2. Order any supplies you need for reception: matches, napkins, guest book, extra serving pieces, ash trays, linens.
3. Obtain marriage license.
4. Pick up tickets for wedding trip and make any final arrangements.
5. Make sure your wedding outfit is complete and ready to wear.
6. Mail change-of-address cards, if address will change.
7. Make an appointment for a hair styling and manicure.
8. Book professional mover if you need one.

One to Two Weeks before Wedding:
1. Begin to pack household belongings if you are moving.

2. Wrap wedding presents for groom and attendants.
3. Pack for wedding trip.
4. Give caterer final estimated number of guests.
5. Address wedding announcements and, if you will be out of town, give them to someone to mail the day after the wedding.
6. Make a final check with all suppliers to make sure that everything is in order.

PLANNING THE HONEYMOON

In the midst of preparing for the Big Event, don't forget to plan a wedding trip. You probably won't want to go to a "honeymoon resort"—one has to be very young and very naive to indulge that fantasy. And fortunately, no one has yet come up with the idea of honeymoon resorts for remarried persons. But you should think about a wedding trip where the two of you can relax and start off your new life together alone, especially since a large part of the prewedding activity will obviously have centered around your children and families.

Although a trip after the wedding that is not officially a honeymoon may seem simple enough to handle, tensions will be running high and you will want everything to go smoothly and be relaxing. The best way to insure that this will indeed be the case is to plan carefully in advance. Make reservations, get your documents in order if you are leaving the country, pack before the wedding, make arrangements for your children and tell them of your plans well in advance so they won't feel abandoned. Then take off and have the time of your lives.

Chapter Two

INVITATIONS AND ANNOUNCEMENTS

*O*ne of the first things on the agenda after you decide how large a wedding and reception you want is to plan the invitations and announcements. When you order or select them, you should also choose writing paper for your personal use. You will need some stationery to use for invitations (if you plan to write them yourself), some paper for thank-you notes for gifts and parties given in your honor, and some paper for thank-you notes and other correspondence after the wedding, if you plan to change your name.

NAME CHANGES—THE BIG QUESTION

Just ten years ago, a woman who got married—whether for the first or the fifth time—automatically took on her husband's name. The rare woman who had a professional name was still Mrs. John Smith socially—and that was the name she used in all her social correspondence.

Today, there is a growing trend for women not to change their names when they marry. Many women who married several years ago took their husband's names, divorced, and then worked under their married names. Sometimes they do not change their names when they remarry but, rather, they keep their first husband's surname, which is used with their own first and middle names or with their first and maiden names.

The name you choose to use is a highly personal matter, but there are some guidelines to help you decide which name to use on your wedding invitations and on your social stationery.

If you use a professional name, but do not consider it your social name, then you should use the name you use socially on your invitations. If, for example, you are known professionally as Pam Wheeler but socially as Pam Wheeler Baker, your divorced name, then you should use Pam Wheeler Baker on your wedding invitations. If you have, on the other hand, resumed the use of your maiden name, then you use Pam Wheeler on your wedding invitations.

You should have your personal stationery printed or engraved with the name you plan to use socially. If you will be retaining the name you used before marrying—either Pamela Wheeler or Pamela Baker or Pamela Wheeler Baker—then that is the name that you have printed on your writing paper. If you will retain your own name at work but take your new husband's name socially, then your married name will be Mrs. Jeremy Smith, or the newer form that many married women prefer, Pamela Smith.

Announcement of the name that you plan to use is usually done informally, mostly in conversations with friends and acquaintances, and the name you have printed on writing paper that you use after your marriage is also a clearcut clue to others regarding what you expect to be called.

DECIDING WHOM TO INVITE

Once you have resolved the use of your name, you have to decide whom you want to invite to the wedding and/or reception before you can order the invitations. Deciding whom to invite to this wedding will probably be an even stickier job than planning for your first wedding. At your first wedding, your major concern was probably persons whom you omitted due to lack of facilities or because they lived so far away that you didn't want to obligate them to a gift. At this wedding, you will be dealing with more complex relationships and a far more confusing set of emotions.

If you choose to have a private wedding with only yourself and your groom, or with your parents and possibly your children and a couple of good friends to stand up for you, no one can possibly criticize this. Even if you have a large reception, you can (and many persons who marry again do) have a very small and private wedding.

Ex-spouses, regardless of how many children you share or how congenial your relations are, are never invited to the wedding. Your ex-inlaws are another matter. If you have children, your ex-inlaws may have remained close to you. An ex-sister-in-law may well be an old friend or roommate from college days. The best way to decide whether or not to invite such persons is to first evaluate *your* feelings and then to ask others about *their* feelings.

Begin with yourself. Do you want your ex-mother-in-law present, even if she is a close friend? The chances are that you will not. And the thing to do is to not invite her; most likely, she'll understand without your saying anything. If you have considered your feelings, and you feel comfortable extending an invitation to ex-relatives, then you must still ask them how they feel. Don't assume that they will want to be present; more than likely, they will not, even if they have remained dear friends with you.

As a rule, ex-relatives will assume that they will not be invited to this wedding, and you will not need to say anything. If you feel you must discuss this with them, you should state your feelings clearly, and don't let someone else's feelings change your mind. The last thing you want is memories of your first wedding haunting this one, and you are the only person who can decide who will be too close for comfort.

You can keep the wedding as small as you like and then invite as many persons as you like to the reception. But you should invite everyone who attends your wedding to the reception. At one particularly lovely wedding, where both the bride and groom had been married before, thirty friends attended the late afternoon ceremony and then adjourned to the apartment the couple shared for a champagne and hors d'oeuvres reception. Several hours later, after their friends had left, the couple and their immediate families continued the celebration with a luxurious dinner at a fine French restaurant.

WHO ISSUES THE INVITATIONS?
Unlike the first wedding, where the parents of the

bride nearly always have the pleasure of extending the invitations, a bride or a bride and groom often choose to issue invitations in their own names, especially if they are responsible for planning the wedding. A wedding invitation may also be issued by any relative of the bride; by one or both of her divorced parents; by a surviving parent, if one parent is deceased; by a surviving parent and that parent's new spouse; or by a close friend of the family or of the bride. The wording of the invitation varies according to who is issuing the invitations. Samples of various invitations are shown later in the chapter.

KINDS OF INVITATIONS

Since most persons getting married again plan an informal wedding and invite a fairly small number of guests, the most popular ways of issuing invitations are by handwritten note, by telephone, or by telegram or day letter, but printed or engraved invitations are also acceptable.

Handwritten Invitations

Of the three methods, a handwritten note is by far the nicest touch. They can be used for any informal wedding, in which the guest list is small enough for you and possibly your mother and a friend to handle writing all the invitations. All the invitations should be written in the same wording. For example, if your mother is sponsoring the wedding, even if you write the invitations, you write them as if you were your mother. One technical difference between a formal, engraved invitation and an informal handwritten one is that the hostess rather than the host and hostess officially issues this invitation. In practice, though, many hostesses issue the invitations in their own and their husband's name.

Choose any pretty and appropriate stationery on which to write the invitations. White or pastel colors are most appropriate, and paper with small drawings or other artwork is not considered in good taste. You may use paper that is printed or engraved with the name of the person issuing the invitations. You cannot yet use your new name, if you are planning a name change. Use regular-sized writing paper or small folded note paper.

If the address is printed on the paper, there is no need to state it again in the invitation; simply say that "John and Mary are being married at home." An R.s.v.p. is never used on a handwritten note; you must assume that invited guests will respond to your invitation.

Here is a sample of a handwritten note issued by the mother of the bride:

Dear Aunt Martha:
   Jeremy and Pam are being married at my home on Wednesday, June 20, at 5 P.M. We are planning a buffet supper right after the ceremony. I do hope you and Uncle Tim will be able to join us and help to celebrate our happy event.
                              Love,
                              Lillian

Here is a sample invitation issued by a bride-to-be:

Dear Aunt Martha,
     I am being married to Jeremy Smith next Wednes-
day, June 20, at the apartment, 231 West End Avenue,
in New York. I hope that you and Uncle Tim will be
able to join us for the ceremony at 5 P.M. and for cake
and champagne afterward.
                                        Love,
                                        Pam

An invitation being issued by the bride and groom
might read as follows:

Dear Aunt Martha,
     Jeremy and I are getting married next Wednesday,
June 20, and we hope you will be able to join us for the
ceremony and for champagne and cake afterward. The
wedding is scheduled for 4 P.M., 231 West End Avenue,
apartment 1301.
                                        Love,
                                        Pam

As you can see, it is rather difficult to issue a truly
joint wedding invitation since one person obviously
writes and signs the note. If you feel strongly about
sharing, you might do what one couple did and invent
your own semiformal invitation. This couple bought
unprinted manila cards of the type that are ordinarily
used for formal wedding invitations, and in black ink
they wrote the following:

A Wedding Celebration
Please join us for our wedding
and for refreshments afterward.
Pam Wheeler Baker and Jeremy Smith, Junior
4 o'clock
231 West End Avenue
Apartment 1301
New York
R.s.v.p.

Telegrams and Day Letters
Telegrams and day letters, the latter being less expensive, are another way to issue invitations to an informal wedding. A bride might wire her friends and the groom might wire his. Either way, they could use the same message, for example:

JEREMY AND I BEING MARRIED THURSDAY, JUNE 21, AT 8 P.M. IN QUIET CEREMONY. HOPE YOU AND UNCLE TIM WILL JOIN US.
LOVE, PAM.

An invitation issued by the mother of the bride or anyone else might be worded

PAM AND JEREMY BEING MARRIED TUESDAY, JUNE 19, AT 8 P.M. IN QUIET CEREMONY AT OUR HOME. HOPE YOU CAN ATTEND.
LOVE, LILLIAN.

Again, with a telegram or day letter, you cannot request a reply, but can only hope that the recipient will know enough to respond or will pick up your clue that few persons are being invited from the words "in quiet ceremony."

Telephone Invitations

The least formal, but equally acceptable, way to issue invitations is by telephone. If the guest list is small, the person who is issuing the invitations—usually the bride and groom or the mother of the bride—makes all the calls. If it is too large for one person to handle, the task may be delegated, but the caller still issues the invitation in behalf of the person planning the wedding. A friend calling for the bride might say, "Pam asked me to tell you that she and Jeremy are being married at Pam's parent's home next Wednesday in a quiet ceremony. They both hope that you will be able to join them. The ceremony is planned for 5 P.M., and then everyone is going out to dinner afterward." Someone calling for the mother of the bride might say, "Mother asked me to tell you that Pam and Jeremy are being married at home next Wednesday. We hope you will be able to come. The ceremony is at 5 P.M., and then we would like everyone to join us for dinner afterward."

One advantage of issuing invitations by phone is that you usually get an immediate response or at least the caller feels obliged to call you back with a definite answer. Telephone calls usually are used only when the wedding is planned on such short notice that there is no time to write notes.

Printed or Engraved Invitations

Invitations to a formal or large wedding may be printed or engraved. Of the two, engraving is always the nicer, but it is also more expensive, and printing is perfectly acceptable. Traditionally, such invitations are issued on plain white or manila stock, and come with two sets of envelopes. The following illustrations show how to place the invitations in the envelopes.

WORDING OF FORMAL INVITATIONS

Custom dictates the wording of printed or engraved invitations. The "honor (honour) of your presence" is used for a church ceremony, whereas the "pleasure of your company" is appropriate for a home wedding or one held in a hall or club. The hour is written "half past four" or "half after four"; quarter hours are marked by "quarter past" or "quarter before." Honor can be spelled "honor" or "honour." The state and city are always spelled in full, an equally proper gesture in handwritten notes. Mr., Mrs., and Dr. are the only abbreviations, except for R.s.v.p., that are permitted, and R.s.v.p. is never proper on an invitation to a church ceremony. It can be used only for a social occasion. Miss or Mrs. are never used when your parents issue the invitations, and Miss can be used only for a woman who has never been married before. Mrs. is proper for a divorced or widowed woman who is issuing her own invitations. Ms. which has gained widespread acceptance in business, is rarely seen on wedding invitations. If you don't want to use Miss and you aren't known as Mrs., even though you are divorced, simply use your name without a title before it.

Invitations to Reception Only

If handwritten invitations, phone calls, or telegrams or day letters are used to invite a person to a wedding, any mention of a party or reception afterward should be noted in the invitation. If the wedding will be small and private, but you are inviting many persons to the reception, here is the accepted form for a handwritten letter and for a formal invitation:

Dear Janie,

Jeremy and I are being married quietly with just our families present next Saturday afternoon. At seven, we hope you and Bill will join us for a reception to celebrate the start of our new life together. It's being held at the Talley Club, 40 Fifth Avenue. We look forward to seeing you both.

Love,

Pam

Notice that the letter does not state whether or not dinner will be served, nor does it indicate what dress is expected. The hour usually dictates what the refreshments will be: an afternoon reception calls for tea or light refreshments, and a reception held during the dinner hour, such as 7 or 8 P.M., indicates that a dinner or buffet meal will be served. If you want to avoid serving a full meal, schedule the reception for the afternoon, or for five or six o'clock when guests will expect only cocktails and hors d'oeuvres. The dress is also dictated by the time of day and the kind of invitation—that is, formal or informal.

A formal invitation to the reception only reads as follows:

Mr. and Mrs. Robert Wheeler
request the pleasure of your company
at the wedding breakfast (dinner) of their daughter
Pamela Wheeler Baker
and
Jeremy Smith, Junior
on Saturday, the third of November
at one o'clock
Roundlake Country Club
Jacksonville, Iowa

R.s.v.p.

You can also enclose an invitation to a reception with a wedding invitation. It should read as follows:

> *Reception immediately following ceremony*
> *Four Hills Country Club*
> *333 Fifth Street*
>
> *R.s.v.p.*

Ceremony Card with Reception Invitation

Alternately, if you are inviting only a few persons to the wedding, but are planning a large reception for which formal invitations are being sent, you may decide to enclose a printed or engraved ceremony card. It should be worded as follows and should be half the size of the invitation to the reception:

> *Ceremony*
> *at four o'clock*
> *St. Andrew's Presbyterian Church*
> *455 Fifth Avenue*
> *New York*

The samples that follow show the possible ways of handling wedding invitations under a variety of circumstances.

Bride Issues Invitation. This is also the wording for a formal wedding invitation.

The honor of your presence
is requested at the marriage of
Miss Pamela Wheeler
to
Jeremy Smith, Junior
on Saturday, the third of November
one thousand, nine hundred and eighty
at four o'clock
Central Presbyterian Church
Three Hundred Main Street
Lafayette, Indiana

Divorced Woman Issues Invitation. Although divorced women rarely issue formal invitations, here is the format should you wish to do so:

Pamela Wheeler Baker
requests the pleasure of your company
at her marriage to
Jeremy Smith

Notice that Wheeler is the maiden name and Baker is the woman's first husband's name. If she has legally resumed her maiden name, the invitation would read:

Pamela Wheeler
requests the pleasure of your company

More rarely, an older, divorced woman may issue an invitation that uses her maiden name and her married name combined in such a way as to indicate her divorced status:

Mrs. Wheeler Baker
requests the pleasure of your company

Widow Issuing Invitation. An invitation issued by a widow reads as follows and uses her married name:

Mrs. Donald Ellis Rabb
requests the pleasure of your company
at her marriage to

Bride and Groom Issuing Invitation.

Pamela Wheeler Jones
and
Jeremy Smith
request the pleasure of your company

Divorced Parents Issuing Invitation for Divorced Daughter. Divorced parents may issue an invitation for a divorced daughter together if that is her preference, or either parent may issue the invitation. If the mother is remarried and issues the invitation, it reads as follows:

Mrs. Jackson Connelley
requests the pleasure of your company
at the marriage of her daughter
Pamela Wheeler Baker

An invitation issued by a father would read:

Mr. Donald Wheeler
requests the pleasure of your company
at the marriage of his daughter
Pamela Wheeler Baker

Other Relative or Friend Issuing Invitation. If a close relative or a good friend sponsors your wedding, the invitation should be worded as follows:

Mr. Burke Wheeler
requests the pleasure of your company
at the marriage of his niece
Pamela Wheeler Baker

A friend may sponsor the wedding of a very young woman, who may or may not have been married before, but who usually has not been, or a woman who has no immediate family nearby. A young woman working in the embassy of a foreign country far from her home might permit a good family friend or a boss to sponsor her wedding. The invitation should be worded in the following way:

Mr. Leo Lanson
requests the pleasure of your company
at the wedding of
Pamela Wheeler Baker

When the Wedding Is in the Bride's Home. If the wedding is being held in the bride's home or, as occurs sometimes today, in a home that she is already sharing with the groom, no mention is made of the fact, as it might be if her mother were issuing the invitations for a wedding in her home. Instead the invitations might read:

> *Dear Aunt Minnie:*
> *Jeremy and I are being married next Saturday, June 4, at half past four. We do hope that you and Uncle Bob will be able to join us for the ceremony and for champagne and cake afterward. The wedding will be at 23 East Park Avenue, Apartment 1301. We'll look forward to seeing you then.*
> > *Love,*
> > *Pam*

Aunt Minnie and Uncle Bob, undoubtedly being of another generation, will be more than happy to overlook at whose apartment the wedding and reception are taking place.

Wedding in Club, Restaurant, or Hall. If a formal invitation is issued and the wedding is held in a club, restaurant, or hall, the name of the place is substituted for the line where the name of the church is mentioned.

Formal Invitation to Wedding and Reception. Sometimes an invitation will ask guests to both the wedding and the reception. If so, it is worded as follows:

Mr. and Mrs. Jack Wheeler
request the pleasure of your company
at the wedding of their daughter
Pamela Wheeler Baker
to Jeremy Smith, Junior
and to the reception immediately following
the ceremony
on Saturday, the fourth of June
at four o'clock
23 Park Avenue
Apartment 1301
New York City

R.s.v.p.

ANNOUNCEMENTS AND AT-HOME CARDS

Announcements are sent after a wedding to tell persons who were not invited to the ceremony or reception that you have married again. The news of the wedding is often passed informally, either by handwritten letter or word-of- mouth among friends. You may, if you wish, send a printed or engraved announcement of your exciting news. The year is always printed on an announcement, although it is optional on a wedding invitation. A formal printed or engraved announcement is appropriate regardless of how small or private the wedding was. The form for a printed formal announcement made by the bride's parents is as follows:

> *Mr. and Mrs. Clifton Wheeler*
> *have the honor to announce*
> *the marriage of their daughter*
> *Pamela Wheeler Baker*
> *to*
> *Jeremy Smith, Junior*
> *on Thursday, the twentieth of June*
> *One thousand, Nine hundred and eighty*
> *Lafayette, Indiana*

A couple announcing their own marriage would use this wording:

> *Pamela Wheeler Baker*
> *and*
> *Jeremy Smith, Junior*
> *have the pleasure to announce*
> *their marriage*
> *on Thursday, the twentieth of June*
> *Nineteen hundred eighty*
> *Lafayette, Indiana*

A divorced woman would use the following format:

> *Pamela Wheeler Baker*
> *(alternately: Mrs. Wheeler Baker)*
> *has the pleasure to announce*
> *her marriage*
> *to*
> *Jeremy Smith, Junior*

A widow would use the following format:

Mrs. John D. Baker
has the pleasure to announce
her marriage
to
Jeremy Smith, Junior

If you have so many persons to tell that you don't feel able to write personal letters—and you don't feel comfortable with formal announcements—you can always buy a plain white or manila invitation and hand-write something like this:

Pamela Wheeler Baker
and
Jeremy Smith, Junior
announce with pleasure their marriage
Thursday, the twentieth of June
Nineteen hundred eighty
Lafayette, Indiana

Announcements are mailed the day of or the day after the wedding, at the earliest.

At-home cards, which may be enclosed with a wedding announcement or mailed separately, give the address of a newly married couple. They used to announce the date when formal calls would be accepted, but since formal calls are rarely made today except in diplomatic circles and on military bases, they no longer serve this function. An at-home card today is more likely to serve as the announcement that a marriage has taken place. It should be used to announce a new address; at-home cards are not appropriately sent by a couple who have been cohabiting for any length of time before marrying. An at-home card is printed on white or manila paper and is about one-third the size of the wedding announcement; your stationer can show you various forms. If it is enclosed with an announcement, it must match it in color and type style. Traditionally it reads:

Mr. and Mrs. Jeremy Smith, Junior
321 West End Avenue
New York, New York 10025
after the thirtieth of June

If the at-home card is enclosed with the announcement, it might read:

At home
after the thirtieth of June
321 West End Avenue
New York, New York 10025

A woman who is not assuming her new husband's name might have the following at-home card printed:

At home
Pamela Baker and Jeremy Smith, Junior
321 West End Avenue
New York, New York 10025
after the Thirtieth of June

Alternately, you might choose to send informal announcements of your new address; these can be purchased in any good stationery department or from a stationer.

PLANE/TRAIN CARDS AND MAPS

Sometimes, particularly at a second wedding, a couple will plan the ceremony or reception at a special place that is away from the community in which they live. They may arrange transportation for their guests under such circumstances. In these instances, a train or plane card (mostly a train card, unless money is no problem) is enclosed with the invitation. Here is a sample format:

> A special train will leave Grand Central Station at 3 P.M. and arrive back in New York at 1 A.M. Please present this card to the conductor.

A plane/train card is the size of the invitation, and like the ceremony or reception card, is printed on the same stock, in the same typeface, and in the same color ink as the invitation or other enclosures.

If the site of the wedding or reception is unknown to many guests, you may enclose a printed map providing directions. Purists may object to this enclosure with a formal invitation, but it is far kinder than letting guests fend for themselves in a strange place.

STATIONERY NEEDS

Here is a checklist of your stationery needs when you're planning a new life. You may not need everything on the list, but it offers a good starting point for sorting out what you do want.

☐ Wedding and reception invitations—formal
☐ Wedding invitations—informal
☐ Announcements—formal or informal
☐ Enclosures (plane/train cards, maps, at-home cards, ceremony cards, reception cards)
☐ Note paper for thank-you notes written before the wedding
☐ Informals with your new name or monogram or with your old name or monogram, if you are not changing it
☐ Formal writing paper
☐ Everyday stationery, with your name and address printed on it

A stationer can also supply printed matches and napkins or any other paper needs. He will help you choose a paper stock and select the typeface you want to use.

If you purchase engraved stationery, remember that the die used to engrave your name or monogram will be good for years, so you can easily reorder your papers when the supply runs low.

Chapter Three

DRESSING TO GET MARRIED AGAIN

*T*he single best thing about getting married again is that you aren't a blushing, innocent bride this time. Most of the things that good taste dictates you shouldn't do—such as wearing full traditional wedding regalia—you wouldn't want to do anyway. And even if you can't wear a veil or a long lace bridal dress with a ten-foot train, there are lots of ways to be a stunning bride. And every woman *is* a bride on her wedding day.

At this wedding, you can wear any look you want, create any mood you choose. You can look as innocent, as romantic, or as sophisticated as you want. In short, your only obligation is to make sure that you look as lovely as you possibly can.

A FEW WORDS ABOUT YOUR WEDDING DRESS

A woman who has been married previously usually does not wear a long, traditional, white wedding dress, nor does she wear a veil. On the other hand, you can, if you desire, wear a white long or short dress and wear a delicate hat with a wisp of veiling. Good taste dictates only that you not try to recreate the image of a first-time bride, and that leaves you a lot of freedom in choosing what to wear.

AVOIDING A TOO-BRIDISH LOOK

Here are a few specific hints that will help you avoid looking—even unintentionally—like a first-time bride.

• Avoid an all-lace, high-necked, long-sleeved wedding dress. This is the one style in the world that always looks like a first-time bride. A lace suit or dress that is cut lower or has short sleeves, however, is appropriate.

• Choose a pastel or a white over a pastel fabric or a light beige rather than a pure white. (There is another reason for doing this: unless you are a very young blushing bride, white probably isn't your best color, anyway.)

• If you do choose an all-white dress—and you certainly should if that is what you look stunning wearing—add a note of color somewhere—your bouquet, a sash, a colored shawl, a jacket, or a purse.

• Consider a bridesmaid's dress. They invariably have a festive, feminine look that stops just short of looking too bridish.

• Consider some of the less traditional wedding dress styles that many brides have taken to wearing in recent years. For example, you might wear an Indian sari, a Mexican wedding dress, or an antique dress.

• Deliberately choose something slightly more daring than you might if you were eighteen and innocent. It's your privilege. You can wear a dress that is a little more low cut or cut in an unusual way, if that is what you choose to do.

Before choosing any kind of dress, however, be sure

to check with the clergyman who will be marrying you. He may not be comfortable with a white dress or a dress with short sleeves or a low neckline. Some religions have restrictions, too, that may affect your choice of a wedding dress.

CHOOSING A WEDDING DRESS

When deciding what kind of wedding dress you want, you have to consider what you can afford, how formal the wedding or reception will be, and what mood you want to create. One woman we know used her wedding gown to set the entire mood for her wedding and reception. She chose a white lace over pink satin street-length dress. It had a seductively low V-neck and full, gathered sleeves that offset the daring neckline with a touch of innocence. She carried a small nosegay of tiny wild flowers tied with pink ribbons. The tablecloths, napkins, and other accessories at the reception were the same shade of pink as her dress. Her single attendant wore a pink piqué suit and a white lace blouse. Both women wore small cocktail hats, and the bride's hat had a bit of veiling attached to it with a small pink rose. Just as this woman's dress set the theme—romantic and somewhat mysterious—for her wedding and provided most of the atmosphere, so can any dress you choose. Furthermore, this time around your primary concern is to look like a beautiful woman. Even many first-time brides, if they had the freedom to do so, would opt for this rather than for the costume feeling that so many traditional wedding dresses convey. The drawings that follow offer some suggestions on styles that are appropriate when you are getting married.

THE FORMALITY OF YOUR DRESS

A wedding can be ultraformal, formal, semi-formal, or informal. Ultraformal weddings are the province of the first-time bride, but anyone who has gone through one usually finds that one is enough. They take a lot of planning and have caused more than one bride to lose perspective on the joys of getting married.

Any of the other three types of weddings is fine for someone who is getting married again. For a formal wedding, the bride wears a long, simple wedding dress or an evening dress. Guests also wear evening clothes.

At a semiformal wedding, the bride wears a dressy short or long dress, usually in a simpler fabric and style than is found in an evening dress. The groom wears a dark suit.

At an informal wedding, usually the kind that takes place in city hall or in a judge's chambers, the bride wears a nice street outfit, often with a hat and gloves, and the groom wears a suit.

SHOPPING FOR YOUR WEDDING DRESS

Shop early even though you aren't looking for a traditional wedding dress. A wedding is a nice time to splurge on a designer's dress, and you will want to leave time to order the color you look best in and to make any necessary alterations. And if you do choose a wedding dress or a bridesmaid's dress, you will need to order it in advance. Bridal dresses take six to twelve weeks for delivery. During the busy bridal seasons, Christmas and June through August, they may require more than twelve weeks.

When you shop for your wedding dress, apply the

kind of makeup you would expect to wear with the dress. You will probably want to adjust your makeup after you have chosen the dress, but you should wear a little more than your work-a-day makeup while shopping.

Carry heels of the height that you will want to wear and wear them as you try on dresses. Bring or wear any underwear that may be needed for a dress. If you plan to wear a girdle, wear one the day you shop. Be sure, too, to bring along several types of bras—a strapless, one that is low cut, and possibly a halter-style bra.

One very busy career woman we know managed to choose her wedding dress and clothes for her new life all in one day. To do this, she used the personal shopper at a store where she regularly shopped. She simply called the shopper and explained what her needs were and what kind of dress she was hoping to find to be married in. The personal shopper made a few suggestions, pulled a selection of clothes for her, including a dress that was perfect for the wedding and reception. In one shot, the woman had solved most of her clothing problems—she had only to accessorize her wedding dress, a task that she found very easy and pleasurable, mostly because she had made everything else so simple.

A saleswoman can be a great help when you are shopping for a wedding dress. Tell her that you have been married before, and explain you don't want to look like a first-time bride. Indicate the mood you hope to convey—romantic, Victorian, sophisticated, whatever. Indicate whether you want a white dress or are hoping to find a pastel or print dress.

You also need to keep in mind the fabrics that you

will find during each season. Aside from year-round synthetics, acceptable winter fabrics for formal dresses include crepe, lace, taffeta, satin, peau de soie, brocade, velvet, and chiffon. Summer fabrics include chiffon, organza, linen, dotted Swiss, piqué, and cotton.

A nice thing about looking for *this* wedding dress is that you have a far wider range from which to choose. You need consider only what is flattering to your figure and face—and what is not. Puffed sleeves, for example, and short sleeves are excellent for showing off very young, firm arms. Loose, long sleeves hide upper arms that are slightly heavy. Bell sleeves balance small hips. You can also choose from a wide variety of necklines. The illustrations that follow show the various choices.

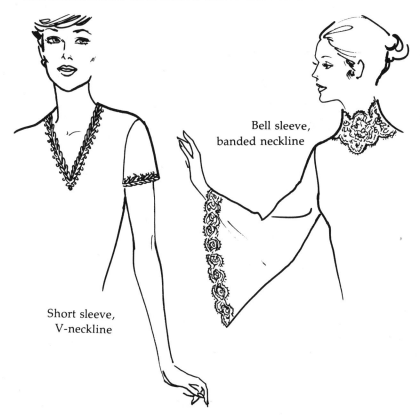

Bell sleeve,
banded neckline

Short sleeve,
V-neckline

Bishop sleeve,
scoop neckline

Baby doll sleeve,
Queene Anne neckline

The length of the dress you wear will depend mostly on the wedding time, but long dresses are not usually worn before 6 P.M. If you wear a street-length dress, its length will probably be dictated by current style. Remember, though, that you want to look your most alluring on your wedding day, so if midcalf skirts are all the rage, but you don't look your best in them, by all means go ahead and shorten your dress to the length that most flatters you.

ACCESSORIZING THE DRESS

Headpiece. Once you have chosen the dress, the next step is to accessorize it. The first accessory you choose will probably be a headpiece, since you can usually buy that in the same place where you buy your dress. Don't, however, limit yourself to the headpieces in the bridal department if that is where you find your dress. If you want a more sophisticated hat, go to a milliner or a hat department that will have exactly what you are looking for. While you will not want a traditional bridal veil, you certainly can wear a small veiled hat. You can also wear fresh flowers in your hair, or you may choose to be bareheaded. The choice is yours. Generally, choose a hat to match the dress (you can even have one made of the same fabric if you like), but don't be afraid to find something entirely different in color and fabric if you think it looks right. The look of a matching outfit just may not be for you, and matching accessories to your clothes has not been very fashionable for the last few years, anyway. Don't be afraid to choose what suits you or to carry out your own personal look.

Summer hat

Hat band with short veil

Cocktail hat

Flowers in hair

Juliet cap

Lingerie. After you have chosen a hat, head for the lingerie department and buy yourself a complete set of underwear to wear with your wedding dress. This is a time to treat yourself to the loveliest things you can afford. You can match it to your dress or choose a beige or white set, if that is your preference. Just be sure it is lacy and very feminine.

A Wedding Wrap. If you are being married outside or in the late fall or early spring, you may need a wrap over your wedding dress, so plan in advance in case you do have to wear one. Getting caught at the last minute may put you in the position of having to wear something that wasn't meant to go with your wedding dress. If the day is mild, there are lots of possibilities. Buy or make a jacket for your dress. If you can't match it, and there is no reason you should, consider a crocheted or a lace jacket. Or you might buy a shawl to wrap around your shoulders—choose something in the same shade as your dress or think about something in a print color that coordinates with your dress. If spring showers might show up on your wedding day, be prepared with a white parasol or umbrella.

If you are married during the cold, winter months, the news is even better. The solution is to rent a fur— something long, luxurious and, yes, *white*. Where else but on this wedding day are you going to have the opportunity to slip into an elegant long, white fur coat? This is definitely the time in your life to make this small splurge, and it will be small, as fur rental prices are hardly extravagant.

If a fur isn't your style, consider wearing a cape—it

won't crush your dress, and capes have a nice, swingy feel to them. If you wear a coat, make sure it is either slightly longer than your dress or definitely a three-quarter length. A coat only an inch or two shorter than your dress looks sloppy.

Gloves. Depending upon the style of your dress, you may prefer to skip gloves. A long-sleeved dress often looks better without them. A suit or evening dress, however, looks slightly more finished with the addition of gloves. The nicest glove you can buy is white kid, but if some color or other fabric works with the dress you choose, by all means go with that. There is one reason to avoid buying a very expensive pair of gloves—you may want to rip the finger for the part of the ceremony where you exchange rings. If you don't do this, plan to remove your glove at the appropriate moment, and be sure you have bought gloves short enough to remove easily. (If you wear kid, be sure it is lined so it will pull off easily.)

Shoes. If you are wearing street-length clothes, any nice pair of leather shoes—sandal or pump—that works with your outfit is fine. Dressier clothes, of course, call for a dressier shoe—often something in kid or fabric died to match or coordinate with your dress.

Purse. Your purse need not match your shoes, but it should coordinate with them. Consider a small leather purse, possibly a clutch, to wear with street-length clothes. For dressier clothes, choose any interesting evening bag in a fabric or in gold or silver.

Jewelry. Traditionally, a bride wears little jewelry—perhaps an heirloom piece and her engagement ring—and this is one tradition that applies to all brides. Actually, the moment you became engaged, you should have put away any pieces of jewelry given to you by your first husband. Obviously, if they are valuable, you may want to wear them again someday or have them reset, but the period when you are planning your new life is not a time to be thinking about this.

On your wedding day, you wear your engagement ring, if you have one. Remember to switch it to your right hand, however, so you can slip on your new wedding ring. You can also wear an heirloom piece of jewelry. Pearls are always appropriate, as is a small brooch of any kind, dainty earrings, or any suitable piece of jewelry given to you by your future husband. If you wear a family heirloom, it should not be one that you wore on your first wedding day.

Neither the bride nor the groom wears a watch on the wedding day—it's not a day when one counts the hours.

FLOWERS TO GO WITH YOUR DRESS

Once you have chosen what you will wear, give some thought to the flowers that you will carry or wear. Avoid the traditional cascade carried by so many first-time brides and, instead, consider a nosegay, flowers for your hair, or even a traditional corsage that can be pinned to your dress or purse (see drawings). Another possibility is to carry a Bible or prayerbook, either alone or with a single flower. You can buy a white Bible or prayerbook or follow the instructions on pages 60-61 for making a Bible cover.

White flowers are prefectly acceptable, but you also have the freedom to choose any color or any kind of unusual bouquet that catches your fancy. You might also consider carrying a more sophisticated flower than many first-time brides might choose: calla lilies or deep pink or red roses, for example.

When you consider the kind of flowers you want for yourself, think about flowers for your attendant. She, too, might prefer a small nosegay or a sophisticated bouquet rather than the traditional cascade.

BRIDE'S BIBLE COVER

Materials
    fabric to cover Bible (satin, moire, or taffeta)
    lace to cover fabric (optional)
    matching thread
    needle
    iron-on interfacing suitable for fabric you
        have chosen
    1 yard satin ribbon to match fabric
    trimming: ribbon, lace, flowers

1. Measure your Bible: height, front cover, back cover, backbone, and width. To the width, add 4 inches. Buy enough fabric and iron-on interfacing to cover these dimensions.
2. Carefully cut out the fabric to the size of the Bible plus ½ inch all around. Cut the interfacing to the same size.
3. Place the interfacing on the wrong side of the fabric, with its wrong side facing in, and carefully iron it on. Fold over ½ inch of fabric all around and press, as shown in drawing 1.

4. If you are covering the fabric with lace (you can order some to match your dress, if you are wearing a lace dress), glue it to the right side of the fabric. Let dry.

5. Wrap the jacket around the book, make a crease where extra fabric forms flaps around front and back of book. Iron in the creases. Remove cover and lay flat again.

6. Cut ribbon into four pieces, each ½ the height of the book, plus 1½ inches. As shown in drawing 2, attach ribbons to inside of cover and then sew ends together, as indicated in drawing 3.

7. Glue or sew on any trim you have planned. Your Bible cover is ready to use.

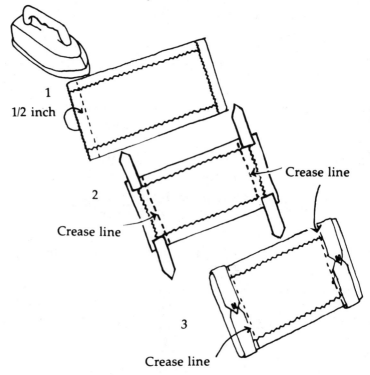

FRAGRANCE

The final touch for any bride—or any woman, for that matter,—is a spray of cologne or a dab of perfume. Even if you have worn one scent for years and consider it your trademark, consider choosing an entirely new scent to wear for your wedding day. The scent you wear should be light and airy, particularly if you are being married during the summer when the combination of a heavy scent and the heat may be overwhelming to you and to those around you. An especially nice treat for yourself is a new line of scents—cologne, bath oil, powder, whatever you want.

CHOOSING YOUR ATTENDANT'S DRESS

Usually you will have only one attendant, but that attendant may well be a young daughter whom you are not quite sure about dressing for this special day. The person who attends you buys her own dress and accessories, so keep this in mind if you choose a bridesmaid dress especially for the wedding.

Your attendant dresses with the same degree of formality you do, and possibly even a little less formally at a daytime or afternoon wedding. If you wear a suit or street clothes, so does she, and she usually chooses something to match or at least not contrast with your outfit.

If you wear cocktail clothes or evening clothes, she should wear something similar. You can wear a pastel solid, for example, while she wears a coordinating print. She can even wear a short dress while you wear a long one, provided her dress is as dressy as yours. That means she shouldn't wear a cotton skirt and top when you are wearing chiffon.

If your wedding is a very dressy event, you may want your attendant to wear a traditional bridesmaid dress. It is a courtesy to choose something she can afford and something she can wear again. Remember, too, that if she buys a dress, she must also accessorize it. It is an especially thoughtful gesture on your part to buy her hat or gloves.

YOUR CHILDREN AS YOUR ATTENDANTS

Children as attendants present no more problem than children do at any other wedding. They, too, should be dressed in keeping with the degree of formality. If your teenage daughter is standing up for you, she should look like your daughter—that means she is more appropriately dressed in something she might wear to a school dance rather than a bridesmaid dress. Younger girls wear Sunday school clothes—their very best. Male children acting as attendants dress much as the groom does, although a very young boy (up to age seven or eight) might wear shorts and a jacket rather than long pants.

GROOM'S OTHER ATTENDANTS

The groom usually has one person who stands up for him, but if very many persons are invited to the wedding, he may ask several friends or relatives to serve as ushers. The groomsmen dress in the same style and color as the groom.

DRESS FOR THE GROOM

There are no restrictions on the groom's dress based on whether or not he has been married before. He simply dresses to suit the formality of the occasion.

For a formal evening wedding, the groom wears a dark dinner jacket with matching trousers, dress shirt, bow tie, and vest or cummerbund. In the summer or in the tropics, the groom may wear a white or light-colored jacket. The groom may also choose a white or light-colored suit for summer, moving into darker shades for a fall wedding. Formal daytime wedding wear includes a gray stroller, waistcoat, striped trousers, shirt, and striped tie. A homburg and gloves are optional. For semiformal and informal weddings, the groom's dress is the same. He wears a favorite—usually solid-colored—suit; white, colored, or striped shirt; and a four-in-hand tie. He may also wear a dinner jacket or formal suit of the type that can be rented from anyone who specializes in wedding apparel. This is often worn with a bow tie and a vest or cummerbund.

FLOWERS FOR THE MEN

Boutonnieres are always appropriate for the groom and his attendants, and they may even be necessary at a semiformal or informal wedding as a means of identifying the ushers. The groom wears a sprig from the bridal bouquet, and the ushers often wear something such as lily of the valley, a rosebud, or a carnation.

ACCESSORIES FOR THE GROOM

The groom wears black shoes and socks with dark pants. Light-colored or dark shoes and socks are worn with light-colored pants. The groom and the groomsmen should take care not to wear colored underwear under light trousers, and briefs rather than shorts should be worn under light-colored trousers.

DRESS FOR THE FAMILIES
OF THE BRIDE AND GROOM

Usually, unless the wedding is quite formal, the parents of the bride and groom do not wear anything special that denotes their roles as parents. They certainly will want to look their best at the wedding, but they do not, after all, stand in the receiving line, nor does the father of the bride give her away at this wedding.

A thoughtful bride and groom will arrange for boutonnieres and corsages for the fathers and mothers respectively, and if grandparents will be present, there is no doubt but that they will also appreciate the special attention that flowers signify.

The families do, as do all the guests, dress to suit the formality of the occasion. If evening clothes are called for, they should wear their best. If street clothes are being worn, then the mother of the bride should resist the temptation to appear in a long dress or anything other than her finest street clothes.

THOUGHTS ON A TROUSSEAU

A trousseau usually refers to a new wardrobe, collected by a young bride, who will only begin wearing her new clothes on the day after her wedding. It is fitting and often quite necessary for the woman who may have just completed her education and who may indeed need an entirely new set of clothes for her new life. Most brides who have been married before, on the other hand, already have established social lives. They often have extensive wardrobes for work and social life. This is no reason, though, for you not to treat yourself to some new things in honor of your new life, and if your life will change at all, you may need some special clothes.

When considering clothes you need, don't think only in terms of your life after the wedding. Consider any entertaining that will be done in your honor before the wedding. How dressy are dinner parties in your circle of friends? Will you need casual clothes? Cocktail clothes? Formal evening wear?

Then consider your wedding trip and any special clothes you may need for that. Will you be dressing for dinner? What about any special sports clothes you may need? You will probably want a couple of new outfits for these special occasions.

You must also consider your new life. Will you continue working or will you retire to take care of children or to do something else? Think about the clothes you will need for this and plan your wardrobe accordingly.

A FINAL WORD

Once in a while a woman who was married very quietly the first time feels slighted that she has never had the opportunity to wear a traditional wedding dress. She hopes to make up for this at her next wedding, and is disillusioned to learn that a veil and long train are not for her. She need not despair, for there is a solution. She could, of course, defy tradition and buy herself an elaborate wedding dress and long veil. But it will cause raised eyebrows, and some persons won't know that she is fulfilling a fantasy. A better solution is to compromise. If you really want a veil, look for a sophisticated hat with a veil attached. You have only to avoid the obviously bridish veils, but there is nothing wrong with having a veiled headpiece. If you really want a train, have a dress made with a train, but choose one that is sophisticated, a dress that might have a train even if you weren't getting married in it.

Your wedding day—be it your first or your fifth—should be a day when your dreams are fulfilled. If you want to stretch the rules of etiquette a little, there is no reason for you not to do so on this special day.

SOMETHING OLD, SOMETHING NEW

Something old, something new
Something borrowed, something blue
And a lucky sixpence in her shoe.

What bride doesn't think of this old rhyme as she is dressing for her wedding? Its origins are unknown, as is whether it is luck, money, or fertility that the words are supposed to bring you. Still, they are a nice custom for any bride. So by all means carry out these old traditions, although the sixpence these days is more likely to be a dime.

Chapter Four

PLANNING A
CHURCH WEDDING

There is no reason that you cannot be married in a church if you want to be, and if the church you choose to be married in is willing to remarry you. Various religions, as noted later, have restrictions about remarriage.

Consult with a clergyman as soon as you decide that you would like a church ceremony. One of the first questions you will settle with him is where you will be married. Since you will probably not have a huge, formal ceremony, you have the option of being married in the main sanctuary; the chapel, if there is one; or in the rectory, which is the clergyman's office. When you talk with the clergyman, find out first whether or not he can and is willing to marry you. If you are a divorced person and he is not willing to marry you, you have two choices: either look for another church to be married in or have a civil ceremony. While the tradition of getting married in one's home church is a strong one, many couples today choose to be married in the community where they live rather than returning to their parents' communities. For this reason, you may not feel as close a tie as you might to a church where you attended Sunday school as a child, and you may decide to look for another clergyman who is willing to marry you if one refuses to do so. This is certainly nothing to be embarrassed about; the worst thing that will happen to you is that a clergyman will decline to marry you because you are not a regular member of his church, at which point you can either join or continue your search. When you meet with the clergyman, there are several other questions and matters to check out. Find out when the church is available, what rules or restrictions exist on music, flowers, photos, and how you can dress.

CHOOSING THE WEDDING DATE

In some religions, the days when you can be married are restricted; usually you cannot be married on Jewish high holidays or the Jewish sabbath, and Catholics rarely marry during Lent; if you do, the wedding is quiet. Most Christian weddings are scheduled for Saturday, but this is largely a matter of convenience for working persons.

The hour is determined by local custom and sometimes by when the church is available. A nuptial mass in a Catholic church is often held in the morning, and other Roman Catholic weddings are also often held around 11 or 12 A.M. In the East and the Midwest, the most popular hours for a wedding are 4, 4:30 or 5 P.M.; Southern weddings are often held around 8 or 9 P.M.

RELIGIOUS RESTRICTIONS ABOUT REMARRIAGE

Each religion has some restrictions about the remarriage of divorced persons and, within each religion, restrictions may vary with the individual clergyman. Here are the general guidelines.

Eastern Orthodox. Divorced persons can remarry three times, but they must have received a church separation in addition to the civil divorce.

Judaism. Wedding procedures vary, depending upon the denomination. Orthodox and Conservative rabbis require a religious divorce in addition to a civil one; some Reform rabbis will dispense with this. A widower is expected to wait seven days before remarrying; a widow or divorced person, three months. Divorced persons may remarry in less time if they are remarrying their former spouses.

Roman Catholic. Divorced persons cannot remarry unless they have obtained an annulment of their previous marriage from a church court.

CHOOSING THE MUSIC FOR A CHURCH WEDDING

Once you have met with the clergyman and settled on the date and time, you should meet with the church organist to discuss music. Acceptable wedding music varies from church to church, and individual clegymen also have their preferences, but usually music is played during the period when guests are arriving, at the start of the ceremony, and for the recessional. Occasionally, music is played after the ring exchange; this is when a soloist often sings. Since there is usually no processional for a remarriage, there is no need to choose music for it, but you should arrange for a piece of music that announces the start of the ceremony. It may begin when the clergyman and groom walk in, or it may be played as the bride enters the church from the side.

If you are planning a processional, good taste requires that you not use the traditional bridal wedding marches such as the "Wedding March" from Mendelssohn's *Midsummer Night's Dream* or the "Bridal Chorus" from Wagner's *Lohengrin*, which is popularly known as "Here Comes the Bride." Before you spend any time regretting that you can't have this music, it may help to know that most church musicians don't think these pieces are appropriate for a wedding anyway, since they are secular music. Most church musicians are delighted to offer you a selection of other very lovely pieces of music, and you can also talk with a local librarian to see what might be appropriate or consult a book called *Write Your Own Wedding* (see page 00 for publishing details) that contains a good selection of interesting classical and contemporary musical pieces suitable for a wedding.

Although you will probably consult with the church organist or music director initially, you may choose to have something other than organ music. The organist or music director can probably suggest a pianist or some other musician who would be happy to play for your wedding. The only disadvantage is that the fees may be higher; you generally leave $30 to $100 for the church musicians; if you hire outside musicians, you may find yourself paying union wages.

TAKING PHOTOGRAPHS

Especially if you are being married in a church, synagogue, or temple, you may want to hire a professional photographer. Formal wedding portraits are not usually taken of the bride since she is not wearing a wedding dress and veil. As a substitute, though, you might consider sitting together for a portrait shortly before or after you are married. Many persons who are remarrying also ask a friend or amateur photographer to handle the pictures. Remember that for this wedding, you—the bride and groom—are the host and hostess, so you should not vanish for any length of time to take pictures. You especially should not hold a photo session at the altar while your guests are waiting for you at the reception. If you want posed pictures of you and your wedding party, take them before the ceremony (and before the guests arrive) or later, at the reception. Here's a list of photographs that are appropriate for a wedding:

Before the Ceremony
    Bride in dress
    Bride with parents
    Bride with honor attendant
    Bride leaving house
    Groom alone
    Groom with best man
    Groomsmen

At the Ceremony
    Guests outside church (other site)
    Bride's family getting out of car
    Ushers escorting close relatives
    Groom's parents being seated
    Bride's parents being seated
    Maid or matron of honor
    Children

Groom meeting bride
Altar or canopy during ceremony
Bride and groom exchanging vows
Ring ceremony
The kiss at the altar
Bride and groom coming up aisle
Bride and groom on church steps
Bride and groom getting into car
Bride and groom in back seat of car

At the Reception
Bride and groom arriving
Bride and groom getting out of car
Bride and groom greeting guests
Bride and groom among guests, wedding party
Buffet table
Bride and groom at bride's table (if there is one)
Bride and groom dancing
Bride and her father dancing
Groom and his mother dancing
Bride and groom talking to guests
Bride and groom cutting the cake
Bride and groom feeding each other cake
Bride and groom toasting
Bride and groom saying good-bye to parents
Bride and groom ready to leave

ARRANGING FLOWERS

Church flowers are usually kept fairly simple, and this is especially suitable when you have been married before. Usually, flowers are placed on either side of the altar, in vases or as part of a floral arrangement on a candelabra. If candles are part of the floral arrangements at the church, they should be lighted during the ceremony. This is a nice thing for your children to do, and if you have no children, you might ask a young relative or friend's child.

More elaborate floral arrangements are permissible, and a florist can make suggestions along these lines. The flowers for weddings are traditionally white, but colored bouquets can be striking and especially nice for this ceremony.

USING THE CHURCH

Because the guest list is often small, only a section of a large church may be used. The drawing that follows shows how this can be done if the bride and groom both enter from the front of the church rather than having a processional. Defining the area of the church that will be used is often done by roping off the used sections with greenery, flowers, or cords, and turning off the lights in other parts of the sanctuary. If there are two aisles, only one is used, even if you have a processional and a recessional. The aisle that is not being used is not decorated, and, if possible, the lights are turned off.

SEATING THE GUESTS

One of the nicer things about getting married again is that seating of guests on either the bride's side or the groom's side can be dispensed with, in part because many of your friends are mutual and because the imbalance could become obvious at a small wedding.

If only twenty or thirty persons are invited, they can probably seat themselves. If you don't use an usher, you should be sure to have the area where you want the guests to sit roped off in some way. It is nice to have someone—a good friend, the best man, a brother—greet the guests and tell them to take a seat anywhere in the roped-off area.

If you have invited more than thirty persons, you will probably need an usher. As a general guideline, an usher is needed for every fifty to seventy-five persons invited. The usher can be someone official, who dresses as the rest of the bridal party does, or he can simply be a friend or one of your brothers who volunteers his services. You may need to help him brush up on his duties. For example, when a man and woman enter together, the usher offers his arm to the woman and escorts her down the aisle; they are both followed by the man. When escorting two women, the usher offers his arm to the one who is obviously older. When escorting two women of the same age, he usually offers his arm to the one who steps forward first. The other woman follows. At a small wedding, if a guest spots a friend or relative, the usher may ask the guest if he would like to sit with the persons he or she greeted, or the guest may even indicate this to the usher. Most of the guests should be seated near the front, with the back pews being filled by late-arriving guests. The very front pews, however, are reserved for the immediate members of the bride's and groom's families. Be sure to tell the usher how many pews should be reserved for your families and who will be sitting in them; these pews might be marked in a different way from the others. If most of the pews have greenery ropes hanging from them, then add colored ribbons or switch to a flowered rope for the two or three pews that are reserved for family.

The members of your immediate families who sit in the specially reserved pews include your parents, sisters and brothers, grandparents, and any other relatives to whom you feel close.

Since there are no sides for guests, both sets of parents can sit together in the first pew or the bride's parents can sit in the first pew and the groom's parents in the second. Alternately, you can open the first few pews across the aisle for the groom's family. This may be necessary if either of your parents are divorced or separated and will not be sitting together.

The seating of divorced or separated parents must also be ironed out in advance. If divorced parents are on friendly terms, and it would be natural for them to sit together, they may. If they are not on good terms, the front pew goes to the bride's mother, and her father sits one or two pews behind. (The same applies for the groom's parents.) If your parents have both remarried, they often attend the wedding and reception without their respective spouses, but this is a personal matter. If the man your mother married was like a father to you, you will naturally want him present at your wedding, and he will probably sit with your mother. And if your father, and possibly a stepmother, reared you, then they might take the front pew, and they will probably want to sit together. Unfortunately, there are no hard-and-fast rules about this; you simply have to play the situation by ear and try to avoid hurting anyone's feelings or making anyone feel ill at ease.

ARRIVING AT THE CHURCH

You and the wedding party should arrive at the church fifteen to twenty minutes before the ceremony; earlier, if you don't want to see anyone before the wedding. The wedding party—bride, groom, and attendants—may all arrive together, the bride and groom may arrive together, or everyone may arrive separately. Since the bride will rarely be living at home, she probably won't make the traditional arrival with her father, although if she has spent the night with her family, she may arrive with them. If you do not drive your attendants to the church, make sure they have transportation, particularly if they are going to be carrying a change of clothes. This means that if you and the groom treat yourselves to a limousine on your wedding day, if possible, you should pick up your attendants and convey them to the wedding in it.

STARTING THE CEREMONY

Arrange for music to be played for about thirty minutes prior to the ceremony while guests are arriving. The music should quicken at the start of the ceremony. If there is no processional, the arrival of the clergyman from the side of the church marks the official start of the wedding ceremony. The bride and groom and their attendants may enter with him, although this is done more often when you have no attendants. If you each have attendants, the more common procedure is for the clergyman, groom, and best man to enter from the side. The music then changes pace, and the bride and her attendant enter, either from the side of the church or by walking down the aisle. A woman who has been previously married traditionally does not have a processional, but these are becoming more common, particularly if the wedding is held in a chapel or small church with a short aisle and the bride has an attendant. It's sometimes a lonely walk for a bride alone, and if you don't have an attendant, this is something to think about when considering whether or not to have a processional.

If you do have a processional, your attendant walks about five feet ahead of you down the aisle. You both hold your flowers at about waist height. Walk slowly and decorously, but do not use the halting step that is sometimes used at a large, formal wedding. Traditionally, the processional music is slow and formal, whereas the recessional music is faster and more upbeat. This is so everyone will have a chance to watch the bride, dressed in her wedding costume, make an entrance. Since you will not be dressed in a traditional wedding dress and veil, and since the Wagner and Mendelssohn pieces are not in good taste, you might discuss with the church organist playing a fairly fast-paced piece of music. You don't want anything swingy, but you also aren't making the solemn grand entrance that you did at your first wedding.

If you have a processional, your children or his children may participate. His children, particularly if they are boys, may want to walk in with him from the side of the church. Your children may want to join you in the processional, especially if they are girls, or you could have all the boys enter with him and all the girls go down the aisle with you. You are probably forming a rather comical picture of hoardes of your children and his surrounding you both during the ceremony. Admittedly, having all your children attend you is not traditional, nor is it likely to be found in any etiquette book. It serves its purpose, though, in terms of making the children feel a part of this special day, and on the few occasions when I have seen exceptions made to accommodate children, I have only found the experience to be touching. Sometimes making everyone feel important and needed is more important than following a rulebook—and I feel that this is one of those times.

EXCHANGING VOWS

As soon as you have reached the altar, the clergyman begins to talk. Every religion has its own ceremony, and increasingly today, clergymen permit persons getting married to supply their own vows if they choose to do so. A section later in the chapter talks about how to write your own vows.

If you follow the traditional ceremony, it is the same for this wedding as for your first, except that the part about the bride being given in marriage is omitted. If you feel strongly about any of the wording of the traditional ceremony—the promise to obey bothers many modern women, for example—talk this over with the clergyman. He will probably be willing to omit any phrases you dislike.

EXCHANGING RINGS

Your honor attendants may hold your rings for you, or you can carry them yourselves. You may have a double or single ring ceremony, just as you would for a first wedding. Occasionally, today, a couple decides not to exchange rings. Obviously, this should be discussed in advance with the clergyman so that he can plan to omit this from the ceremony. The clergyman will give you specific directions about the ring exchange—whether to hand the rings to him for a blessing, how to give them to each other, and so on.

At one wedding rehearsal I attended, I heard the clergyman tell the couple during rehearsal that if either of them dropped the ring during the ceremony, they were to proceed as if nothing had happened and look for the ring later. At another wedding, when the best man dropped the ring and it tumbled out of sight, the matron of honor quietly and quickly came to the rescue—she slipped off her wedding band and handed it to the clergyman to use. Since there is usually no rehearsal for a small second wedding, the clergyman will probably not tell you what to do if such an emergency occurs, so you had better decide among yourselves before the ceremony.

If you have a bouquet, hand it to your attendant when the clergyman asks about the rings during the ceremony. She, in turn, will hand you the ring if you are not wearing it. She usually holds the flowers until the end of the ceremony, returning them to you just before you and your new husband turn to leave the altar. After the clergyman has pronounced you husband and wife, you kiss each other, the bride turns to her attendant to take back her flowers, and then bride and groom face the guests and begin the recessional, followed by their attendants, also arm in arm.

In a church wedding, there is nearly always a recessional for the simple reason that a church is a religious house and you do not greet your friends at the altar or along the aisles in most churches and chapels.

Because the wedding ceremony is brief in most religions and is made briefer still at a second wedding without the processional and the giving away of the bride, some couples choose to have a soloist sing or musicians play a special piece during the service. The best time to do this is right after the ring exchange.

RECEIVING YOUR GUESTS

While there is no official receiving line at this wedding, you and your new husband do greet your guests either at the back of the church or at the reception. Receiving your guests at the church is mostly a matter of local custom. If the reception is being held in the church parlor, then you should go there immediately and await the arrival of the guests. If it is being held at another location, you many want to say hello to everyone at the church, or you may whisk yourselves away and greet your guests as they arrive at the reception

A CHAPEL WEDDING

A chapel wedding is exactly the same as a wedding in the main sanctuary of the church or synagogue. It is sometimes easier not to have a processional and recessional in the small confines of the chapel. Often, the bride and groom merely walk out with the clergyman at the start of the ceremony.

Since chapels are usually fairly small, talk to your florist about scaling down any floral arrangements for the altar.

A RECTORY WEDDING

A wedding in the clergyman's office or private parlor is simple to arrange, and this is how some clergymen prefer to marry persons who have been married before. Usually space is limited, so you cannot invite more than ten or fifteen persons at most to the ceremony. There are no chairs; everyone stands during the ceremony, which is brief. There is no processional or recessional for obvious reasons. The bride and groom and their guests gather about ten minutes before the start of the ceremony and enter the rectory together. There are no flowers for decoration—although the bride and her attendant may wear or carry them—and there is no music.

You and the groom turn and receive the guests' congratulations and kisses immediately after the ceremony ends.

A CIVIL CEREMONY

Sometimes a couple goes to city hall or a judge's chambers to be married. The procedure is much the same as for a rectory wedding, although there are no invited guests except witnesses and possibly your parents, who may also serve as witnesses. Street clothes are appropriate, although the bride may carry a small bouquet.

If you know the judge who is marrying you and his chambers are large enough, you may ask more of your friends to attend the ceremony, provided he or she agrees to this.

THE WEDDING REHEARSAL

Rarely is a rehearsal held for a wedding other than the first. It is necessary only if the ceremony will be detailed or long, or if there will be a processional, and even then you may be able to dispense with the rehearsal.

THE MARRIAGE LICENSE

You must obtain a marriage license—often several days in advance of the day you plan to be married. A clergyman cannot marry you until he has the license.

The requirements for a marriage license vary from state to state, but usually you must present your divorce decree and have a blood test. Call city hall or the town clerk to learn what the specific requirements are for your state.

WRITING YOUR OWN VOWS

This wedding is an especially appropriate time to write your own vows. Some couples choose to write their vows and let the clergyman speak them; others want to tell their guests what this marriage means to them personally and what commitments they are making to each other. Some couples choose actually to write their own wedding vows, while others draw on the writings of others to make up their highly personal ceremony.

Before you write your own vows, talk it over with your clergyman to be sure this is agreeable to him. Once

you have decided to go a
ding vows, and once the c₁
do so, he may be able to rec
help you plan your ceremony.
authored by Mordecai L. Bri١
William H. Genne and called W₁
offers suggestions and resources ₓ
tant, Catholic, and Jewish faiths res₍
ing information on this book can b
101 of this book; it is an excellent guid₍
who wants to personalize their wedding b₎
own vows.

A church wedding is quite appropriate,
dled graciously, a lovely way to begin youٵ
together. Many persons who are remarrying s₍
from a church wedding, particularly if they had ٥
first time they married. This is fine, if it is whaٶ
really want to do, but if you want a church weddٵ
then by all means, you should have it.

Chapter Five

❦

GETTING MARRIED
AT HOME

A *home* or garden wedding is always lovely and charming, especially if you have a special or sentimental attachment for the home you want to be married in. Many persons I have talked with over the years have said they would have loved a home wedding, but didn't know how to go about it. So here are the details on how to plan an extraordinarily beautiful home wedding.

WHOSE HOME WILL YOU BE MARRIED IN?

A woman who has been living in her own apartment and who runs her own independent household can always hold the wedding there, if she chooses to do so. She can also get married in her parents' home, even if she has not lived with them for years, or in the home of another relative or a friend. Usually a relative's or friend's home is chosen for its beauty, and the offer of a striking house or apartment, especially for a second wedding, should not be construed as an offer to give the wedding and reception. Accept any generous offer of a home in which you would enjoy being married, but expect and insist on paying your own expenses.

GETTING MARRIED IN THE HOME
YOU SHARE WITH HIM

Many couples who live together before deciding to marry especially want to be married in the home they have created together. Setting all moral judgments aside, this can pose a few etiquette problems. After all, you want your wedding to be a celebration of love, and you want all your invited guests to participate in this in a spirit of caring.

Let's face it, if your parents have refused to cross the threshold of "your" apartment, they won't be happy about the announcement that you are going to be married there. From where they stand, in fact, no matter how delighted they may be with the news that you are "finally" going to marry each other, getting married in an apartment or house where you cohabit may be the crowning blow. After all, not too many years ago, a woman did not even consider living with a man prior to marriage, and the feelings your parents have about your current live-in situation may have more to do with social embarrassment than anything else. If you want your parents to be present at your wedding—and to enjoy themselves—and they have strenuously opposed your living arrangements, then you may have to consider being married somewhere else. Or you might do what one cohabiting couple did and get married in a quiet ceremony in a local church and then return to the apartment for the reception.

The next problem is relatives who may disapprove or feel uncomfortable with your living arrangements.

They, of course, need not be confronted as directly as your parents must be, and there are ways of handling their presence at a wedding in your home. As a start, resist the urge to announce your living arrangements to any relatives who might take offense. If your relatives have any manners at all, they will studiously avoid asking any questions about your living arrangements while they are your guests on your wedding day.

Finally, remove any obvious signs of cohabitation. If this goes against your moral grain, don't think of it as appeasing Great Aunt Minnie, think of it as doing a thorough clean-up before you give a party. You don't really plan to leave his and hers bathrobes draped over the bedroom closet door or your contraceptive foam on the bathroom sink, do you? Wouldn't you put away most such personal effects for any large party? Rather than risk hurt feelings, or worse, a scene on your wedding day, it's safer to remove as many traces of cohabitation as possible.

DRESS FOR A HOME WEDDING

A home wedding can be formal or informal. The bride and groom and their attendants can wear anything from street clothes to evening clothes, with one exception. Because you are being married in your home, you do not wear a hat or gloves. You wouldn't normally wear these things at home, so you don't wear them on your wedding day. You may, if you choose to do so, wear a hat and gloves if you are being married in a garden—they are often a lovely touch.

If you are wearing street clothes, select something that fits in with the intimacy of a home wedding. A suit, for example, might be a little too stiff for the bride, who might better choose a floaty chiffon dress or some other dress that she might wear if she were entertaining in her home on any other special occasion.

THE GUESTS AT A HOME WEDDING

A home wedding can be as large as the number of guests your home can accommodate, but space usually does limit how many persons can be accommodated. Furthermore, anyone invited to attend the ceremony obviously stays for the refreshments later. Technically, you can invite some people to come by for the reception after the ceremony, but to avoid hurt feelings, at a home wedding, usually everyone is invited to both the ceremony and the reception. If the ceremony is held away from the home, you can ask anyone you like to join you later for the reception. A small private wedding and a large reception is a very usual arrangement for a second wedding.

PLANNING THE HOME WEDDING

The first step to planning the home wedding is to decide how to use the space. Obviously, you choose the loveliest spot for the ceremony itself, but you must also decide where to put the coats, where to put the food table, where to serve beverages, and where to put the wedding cake. The best way to do this is to work out a traffic flow chart. Figuring out how your guests will move around the apartment or house often helps you to determine how to use each room or the entire house. Move furniture around—and out—if necessary. You can also rent tables, chairs, a bar, and anything else you need (see chapter 6).

If home weddings are not carefully organized and planned, they can become hectic and out of control at the last minute. To help plan your home or garden wedding, here is a countdown chart showing when to do everything so that you have very little to do at the last minute—the key to successful entertaining for most persons.

COUNTDOWN LIST FOR HOME WEDDING

4 weeks before
> Plan and check supplies and services you will need, using information in chapter 6.

2-4 weeks before
> Consult with suppliers and order everything you need. Try to have as many things as possible delivered before the day of the wedding.

1-2 days before
> Deliveries begin: ice; liquor and other beverages; coat racks, tables, chairs, and other such rented items. Round up anything you are borrowing from friends.

Morning of wedding
> Unavoidable last-minute deliveries and set-ups: flowers, food. Set up coat rack and tables and chairs, etc.

3 hours before
> Check out what hasn't been done and track down anything that is missing. If flowers haven't arrived, for example, make an urgent call to the florist. Inspect all work and make sure everything is done to your taste. Musicians arrive and you talk with them to make any last-minute plans.

1 hour before
> Wedding party gathers to dress, or, if they dress elsewhere, arrive at home where wedding is being held.

30 minutes before
> Music begins and guests begin to arrive.

5 minutes before
> Music changes to signal start of ceremony.

Ceremony begins
> Clergyman walks with wedding party to spot where ceremony will take place.

ARRANGING FOR FOOD

A home wedding is usually more work on your part in the planning and organizing stages, but you should, if at all possible, avoid being burdened with cooking and serving food. If you want to prepare the food yourself, you should prepare foods that are ready to be put on the table and eaten without any last-minute effort on your part. Carrying a ham to the table won't ruin your image as a bride, but passing among your guests with trays of hors d'oeuvres may make you feel like a servant on your wedding day.

The easiest type of food for a home wedding is tea or cocktail food. It can usually be arranged on a table, and guests can help themselves. Slightly more complicated is a buffet where main dishes are served. The guests should be able to sit down to eat, even if only in chairs and sofas with tray tables. Most elaorate is a seated formal dinner. It is easy to see what kind of outside help you need for each kind of meal—you can probably handle a tea or cocktail reception yourself, and you will probably need at least partial catering for a buffet dinner. For a sit-down dinner, you should have full catering and service. Another advantage to hiring the food service is that you won't find yourself doing dishes on your wedding night. Needless to say, no couple should start married life that way.

Using the services of a caterer is probably the best way to handle a seated, formal dinner, but for less formal—and possibly less expensive—food service, consider looking into services offered by delis, cheese shops, gourmet food shops, and bakeries.

When planning the kind of food you will serve, consider the tables and chairs you will need. A sit-down dinner obviously calls for a table large enough to seat all your guests, or a collection of small tables, plus an area from which food can be served. You also may want a small separate table for your wedding cake. At one dinner in honor of some newlyweds, the wedding cake was rolled out from the kitchen on a serving cart festooned with ropes of flowers that were coordinated with real flowers topping the cake itself and strewn on top of the cart. The cake was small, as there were only ten persons at the dinner, and the extra care taken to show it off made it worthwhile and unforgettable.

Since groom's cakes or boxed wedding cakes are not usually ordered for anything but a large, formal reception, here's a suggestion of something else to give as mementos to your guests. Consider having menu cards or even name cards printed with your and your new husband's initials and the date intertwined. Such cards are most elegant when they are printed on white or manila stock with silver, gold, or black ink. If you like, hire a calligrapher to do this for you. A sample follows.

A buffet dinner requires a long table for food service, and, if you can possibly manage it, small tables or tray tables for guests to sit at while they eat. Unlike at a formal dinner, seats are not usually assigned, and there is no official bridal table. The bride and groom simply sit among their guests.

At a cocktail or tea reception, persons eat standing up, but you will need a table for the food and possibly a table for the cake, if it is not used or placed on the main food table. The cake, don't forget, can be a lovely centerpiece.

Sample menus for various kinds of receptions may be found in chapter 7.

MANAGING THE BEVERAGE SERVICE

Unlike a cocktail party where you are expected to offer a variety of drinks, at a wedding reception, it is proper to offer only champagne. If champagne is too expensive, you can serve punch or wine or anything else that fits your budget and taste. It is considerate to have soft drinks and bottled water cn hand for nondrinkers.

Just as the bride won't want to be burdened with serving food at her own wedding, the groom should not have to worry about tending bar. If the caterer won't handle drink service, hire a bartender who will. Often it is cheaper to buy the liquor (and work out a return policy for what you don't use) from your local dealer than to buy it from the caterer or whoever provides the food. Check the Yellow Pages for a bartending school, or if you live near a university, hire students, especially if you are serving only champagne or wine.

CREATING A SETTING

In most church weddings, you can get by with few flowers, if you want to, and let the church itself supply the atmosphere. In a home wedding, though, you need to create the atmosphere, and the easiest and most effective way to do this is with flowers. Florists can do more than create a festive atmosphere, they can also make an altar where none exists, create an aisle, or help to establish the traffic flow. While an aisle is not necessary at a home wedding, a florist can create one with flower ropes, streamers, or judiciously placed plants.

You will almost certainly want to create an "altar," and a florist can be very helpful with this. The simplest method is to use candles and two bouquets, which the clergyman stands between. Even for an indoor wedding, however, you may want something more elaborate such as a trellis or a flower-covered screen. Jewish weddings, which traditionally take place under a chuppa, or canopy, have a natural focal point, and the chuppa is often covered with flowers. This can be an especially beautiful focal point for a home wedding. A florist often can supply a chuppa, a curtain, or some other prop to make an altar.

There are two directions to go in planning flowers for a home wedding. You can strive for a wedding effect—with an altar bedecked with formal floral arrangements and centerpieces for the food tables and other tables. Or you can attempt a less formal look by placing bouquets and informal floral arrangements all around the room. Such bouquets are usually less arranged than a centerpiece is, and they lend atmosphere in a more subtle manner. You could use baskets of flowers or single flowers in bud vases. A creative florist is immensely helpful here. Choose whatever suits your personal taste and the atmosphere in the home where you are being married. If you have modern furniture, for example, a manufactured, flower-bedecked altar may look a little silly, whereas it would be perfect in a home furnished with period furniture.

When you are planning an altar, consider whether or not you will need to kneel during the wedding ceremony. If you will, you need to make some provisions for this—either by obtaining white or pastel satin pillows, two *prie-dieux*, or a kneeling bench. Call the church and ask if they can provide you with anything or suggest where you might order something suitable for your use.

MAKING YOUR OWN MUSIC

If you want live music at your wedding, one drawback to being married at home is that musicians and their instruments take up valuable space. Consider hiring a violinist or any other single musician rather than hiring a quartet, or you might consider using stereo music. You can even use stereo music and have the desired kind of dignified music if you pretape the music for your wedding and reception. To tape your own music, you need only to plan the music you want to use, borrow records from friends or the library, and rent an eight-track or cassette recorder-player if you don't have one. Set-up an afternoon or evening for your recording session, and you can have exactly the kind of music you want for your wedding and reception. It costs about $35 to $50 to rent a recorder-player, or you may be able to use a friend's player.

Your best bet is to use a ninety-minute tape, especially if you want to keep the tape as a memento; longer tapes don't wear very well. If you don't want to save the tape, use a longer-running one. Decide what music you want to use for what part of the day. For instance, if you want fifteen minutes of preceremony music, ten minutes of background music during the ceremony, and then some light music while you and your new husband greet your guests, you must carefully work out the time allotments for each. To make the transition between records, press the pause button on the recorder as one taped segment ends and hold it while you change records on the turntable. You may need some help in doing this. Press the pause button to release it as soon as the new record starts playing.

A local librarian or a friend who is knowledgeable in music may be able to suggest appropriate music to record. There is a book, mentioned earlier, that lists good music for wedding services entitled *Write Your Own Wedding*, by Mordecai L. Brill, Marlene Halpin, and William H. Genne (New York: Association Press, 1973). The book is also an excellent interfaith guide to writing and planning your own wedding ceremony. It costs $3.50 in paper, and can be obtained from Association Press, 291 Broadway, New York, N.Y. 10007, if it is not available through your local bookstore.

PLANNING A GARDEN WEDDING

Essentially, the plans for a garden wedding are much the same as those for a home wedding, except that you cannot count on the weather. The best way to avoid a last-minute upset in your plans is to make an alternate plan should rain ruin your garden wedding. One couple I know simply started the reception early when they saw that a summer shower had temporarily upset their wedding. When the rain stopped an hour later, everyone— in the best of spirits, needless to say—stepped into the garden for the ceremony. After the ceremony, everyone picked up the reception where they had left off.

Few persons are easygoing enough to handle such a loose arrangement, so most persons need a more definite foul-weather plan. The best plan is to schedule an indoor-outdoor wedding. Use the garden and the house. For example, set up the food and drinks inside. If it rains, guests simply move inside. They may be more cramped, but there is no last-minute rush to move the bar and food service inside. Alternately, if the garden is suitable, you can rent a tent and plan festivities under that.

DRESSING FOR A GARDEN WEDDING

A garden wedding can be formal or informal. A garden wedding calls for a soft, flowing dress that appears to be handpicked to coordinate with the garden flowers. Consider a short or long dress of chiffon, organza, or cotton. A floral print or pastel is lovely for a garden wedding, and if you are the type to wear one, a large, floppy hat is the perfect touch. You might also consider carrying a loose spray of flowers—if they don't come from the garden, they should coordinate with the garden's flowers—or a basket of flowers. Let your most romantic fantasies take hold and direct the aura of your garden wedding.

PLANNING THE SETTING

Usually you decide to have a garden wedding because the garden itself is the perfect setting for your wedding. You must still decide where you want to stand during the ceremony. Try to use a feature of the garden—a trellis, a vine-covered wall, a rose bed, a lovely old tree, or anything that is a focal point of the garden.

MUSIC FOR THE GARDEN WEDDING

Planning the music for a garden wedding is much the same as planning music for an inside wedding, except that if you use pretaped or stereo music, you may need to wire the speakers to reach outside. You can, of course, omit music if you want to, but if you decide to rewire the speakers to your stereo, ask a friend who knows how to do these things to help you. This is not a job for an amateur. You can also have live musicians. I once attended a wedding held inside and outside a wonderful old home. The musicians were strolling violinists. If the musicians will be seated, they should be situated on a platform or porch, and they will need chairs. You can rent a wooden platform for the musicians.

THE BEST TIMES FOR A HOME
OR GARDEN WEDDING

It should be obvious from reading this chapter and learning about everything you have to do to organize a home or garden wedding that most garden weddings are held in the early or late afternoon. A garden wedding is always held during the day to show off the garden, but an indoor home wedding could be held at any hour. An 11 or 12 o'clock wedding is followed by a wedding breakfast, although luncheon-type foods are served. An early afternoon wedding is usually followed by a tea or cocktail party, and a wedding held at 6 P.M. or later is often accompanied by dinner.

DANCING

If you have room, dancing is a nice touch at a home

or garden wedding. Inside, you must clear enough space for the dancing; outside, you can rent a wooden platform suitable for dancing.

SEATING

Guests often stand during a home or garden wedding, although you may want to provide chairs for members of the immediate family or for an aged relative. If you do this, don't make one person sit while others stand but, rather, put out chairs for everyone in the immediate family. Chairs provided for the family can be marked off by rope flowers or ribbons. There is no bride's side or groom's side. Guests simply gather around the altar or in front of the clergyman when he appears ready to start the ceremony.

GREETING THE GUESTS

Guests will begin arriving about twenty or thirty minutes before the start of the ceremony. Often the bride and groom mingle with the guests and greet them as they arrive, but if you wish to remain in seclusion until the ceremony begins, then you should ask your maid of honor, your mother, or good friend to greet arriving guests. Someone should be on the lookout for the clergyman and should help him with any last-minute clothing changes or arrangements he needs to make. It is perfectly acceptable when the bride is sequestered until the ceremony for the groom to greet the guests.

THE CEREMONY

There are several ways to start a home or garden

ceremony. The bride and groom may simply walk together to the altar and face the clergyman. The music may be used to announce the beginning of the ceremony by becoming louder, softer, or distinctly religious in tone. Sometimes the bride wants a processional. For some women, this is even a reason to get married at home. A woman who might not feel comfortable walking down a long church aisle alone may relish her slightly smaller-scale moment of glory as she floats down a lovely staircase or enters and walks up a flower-lined aisle. If a processional is planned, then the groom and the best man and clergyman often enter from another room and a shift in the music announces the beginning of the processional. You do need music of some sort if you are planning a processional; it simply doesn't work without it.

There is no recessional in a home or garden wedding, unless the garden is large enough to accommodate one. The bride and groom simply turn and face their guests to receive congratulations. Unlike some church weddings, where the bride and groom may or may not kiss at the altar, they always kiss at the close of a home wedding ceremony. No one else may kiss the bride before the groom does.

Many brides—and grooms—are attached to their homes and feel that they are ideal and lovely places for their weddings. By working with a good florist, and with careful planning, there is no apartment or house too small or too plainly decorated to be turned into a lovely spot for a wedding and reception. And since you will probably want only a few close friends present at this wedding, what could be more meaningful than to be married at home? Years ago, weddings were frequently held in homes and gardens. Home was where life was lived. And today, with the trend toward entertaining ourselves and others in public places, perhaps it is time to consider a return to using the home for life's meaningful ceremonies.

Chapter Six

PLANNING
THE RECEPTION

*T**he* reception you give should look more like a party than a wedding reception. And if you remember the case of nerves—to say nothing of the hours and days and weeks of planning—that went into your first wedding reception, this message can only be a relief to you.

You also have a greater opportunity for variety, which means you can do exactly what you want to do this time around. When your parents were giving you a lavish, ultraformal wedding, you couldn't very well insist on having the reception at your favorite Chinese restaurant, even if that is where you met your fiance and where you spent most of your courtship. Well, this time around, you can plan to have a ten-course dinner at your favorite Chinese restaurant or anything else you want in lieu of a more traditional reception. Not only will none of your friends or family care, but they will probably be delighted to dispense with the ritual that surrounds a traditional wedding reception.

Like other great parties, this one can be planned around a theme. You do need to remember that the purpose of the party is to celebrate your marriage, however, so any theme you choose should be employed with subtlety. One woman of Southern descent planned her wedding for early May and organized it around a Kentucky Derby theme. What made it work was that she carried out the theme only to the extent of serving mint juleps in silver goblets, champagne, and beatin' biscuits and other foods traditionally served on Derby Day. You practically had to be a Kentuckian to discern where the mood for her reception had come from, but this woman was astute enough to realize that once she took away the horse race, she had the trimmings for a pastoral, romantic wedding reception.

Another young woman planned what she called a Bastille Day reception for her early July wedding. She wore white organza, with a blue ribbon at the waist. The tablecloths and other small accessories were blue, and all the flowers were red and white. Instead of a wedding cake, the couple found a French baker to make them a *croquembouche*, the traditional dessert served at French weddings and christenings.

Another woman, who said she didn't consciously have a theme in mind, nonetheless planned a stunning pale yellow wedding for her early fall wedding. The reception was held under a yellow tent, the table decorations, small accessories, and bouquets were all yellow. At the four corners of the tent, she had the florist place topiaries of crisp greens and yellow carnations and daisies. Even the food seemed yellow—curries and an assortment of condiments and a striking yellow and white wedding cake, decorated with still more yellow flowers.

One especially nice thing about this wedding is that you have undoubtedly learned how to give a great party and are more likely to know exactly what you want this time. Just let your fantasies take over when you plan your reception. And don't let yourself be hindered by any "shoulds." You *should* have exactly the kind of party you want for your wedding reception.

NEWLYWEDS AS HOST AND HOSTESS

Since you and your new husband will be giving this party, you need to remember that while you are the stars of the day, you are also the host and hostess. You are responsible for your guests' comfort and well-being. (Of course, if your parents or someone else gives your reception, then you are guests and can act as such.)

While you do not have an official receiving line as you would for a large wedding, you do greet your guests as they arrive. Your parents and even your attendants have no official greeting capacities at this wedding as they would at a large, formal first wedding. This means that they do not stand with you in a formal receiving line. You may, however, ask your attendants to greet the clergyman before the ceremony and to transport him and his wife to the reception or to help in other ways, such as handling guests' coats.

If you and your husband have to leave the reception early because, for example, you have plans to catch a plane, then your attendants or some other good friends may take over your functions as host and hostess. Unlike your first wedding though, you usually do not leave this reception before the last of your guests has departed since you are the official host and hostess. This means that you might do better to plan to leave for your wedding trip the day after the wedding rather than the same day. Persons who come to celebrate your marriage aren't usually inclined to leave early, particularly if they have traveled any distance for the reception.

PLANNING THE GUEST LIST

It is especially common to have a small private wedding and a larger reception. The reception can even be held on another day—when you have returned from your wedding trip, if you like. If you have been living together and wish to avoid any disapproval from your older relatives over having the reception in your home, then holding the reception several days after the wedding is a possible solution.

If the reception is held the same day as your wedding, you must invite everyone who attends the wedding to the reception. And persons may, of course, be invited to the reception who do not attend the wedding.

There is one nice thing about the guest list for a wedding reception. While at other parties you have to take into account whether or not the guests will get along with each other and what they may have in common, for your wedding reception, everyone is expected to get along just because they are there. And what the guests have in common is the desire to celebrate your happiness. You simply ask anyone and everyone whom you want to attend. Old family feuds or personal rivalries are buried in honor of your wedding day.

BEING A GOOD GUEST

There is an art to being a good guest at a second wedding. Aside from the obvious good behavior, which involves arriving early or on time, not bringing uninvited guests, and providing one's own transportation, guests don't reminisce about the bride's and groom's previous weddings. They don't mention ex-spouses and, if the children are absent, they don't ask why they aren't there.

While one is under no obligation to give a wedding gift, most guests will want to give one anyway. Don't ask the bride and groom what they need—if they're polite, they can only discourage your gesture. Just go ahead and buy them something—usually a gift for their home. Avoid the traditional gifts such as toasters and blankets and think in more original terms, such as fine wines, gourmet gadgets or cookware, or anything that takes account of their interests.

CHOOSING THE LOCATION

You can have the reception anywhere you like, including in your own home. Whether you choose your home, a private club or restaurant dining room, or a church basement, go look at the place and figure out how it will work with the number of guests you want to have. Where will you greet your guests? How can you set up tables and chairs, if you want to provide them? Is there room for dancing? Where will you put the coats? Where will the musicians sit? Is there a kitchen? Where can you put the food table? The cake table? Before making a final decision on the place where you will hold your reception, work out the answers to all these questions.

MAKING THE FINAL ARRANGEMENTS

Once you have chosen a place to hold the reception, you have to begin making the final arrangements. Basically, these can be broken down by persons whose services you will need. You need to contact the following persons to help you plan your reception:

Baker
Caterer or some food service group
Liquor dealer
Rental agency (if you will need tables, dishes, linens, or
    silver, and the caterer does not supply them)
Florist
Musicians
Photographer

There is no way to tackle hiring these services except to pick up the phone and make appointments. You may want to peruse magazines for entertainment ideas or use some of the ideas that will be described here and in the next chapter, but try not to have too definite an idea of what you want. A florist may suggest something you hadn't considered, and a baker may have an idea for some delectable desert that would especially suit your fancy. Do explain the mood or theme that you want to convey and, of course, if you know that you want a pink wedding cake and pink flowers everywhere, then that is what you should have.

When planning your reception, try to do as much as you can in advance, so you will have nothing to do on your wedding day but get dressed and enjoy yourself.

Hire as much done as you possibly can. You will need food servers and a bartender, but if you are planning to hold the reception in your home, hire someone to clean it for you—and by all means hire someone to come in and clean up the mess.

Some things—such as arranging the flowers and putting out the food—will have to be left until the day of the party. But again, this is not a day for you to be concerned with these things if you can possibly avoid it. Ask friends to help you or hire someone to handle the last-minute details. Most large cities have professional party organizers, and almost every city has a wedding consultant whose services you can engage if there is a lot of work to be done.

Keep written timetables and checklists to be sure everything is taken care of on schedule. Make lists of what is needed and what you need to do. Keep as little as possible in your head, because while this is a delightful time of your life, it inevitably is a very busy one, and you may forget something very important if you do not write everything down. Here is a list of basic needs for every party:

- [ ] China
- [ ] Silver
- [ ] Glasses
- [ ] Linens (napkins and tablecloths)
- [ ] Serving dishes
- [ ] Trivets, hot trays to keep hot food hot and containers to keep cold food cold
- [ ] Flowes and vases or other containers
- [ ] Candles and candleholders
- [ ] Beverages
- [ ] Ice
- [ ] Mixers and soft drinks
- [ ] Cigarettes and matches

☐ Tables
☐ Chairs
☐ Coat closet or rack and hangers
☐ Guest towels and soap
☐ Cash to pay persons who work for you

For a large group, you may want to rent extra supplies of the following items:

☐ Coat racks and hangers
☐ Extra chairs
☐ Tables for food service or for guests to sit at
☐ Large serving dishes
☐ Coffee server

ORDERING THE BEVERAGES

Since toasting the future happiness and health of the couple is one of the pleasanter ceremonies of life and of wedding days, you will need some appropriate beverages for this purpose. Traditionally, champagne is served at weddings. And although it is expensive, it may cost less in the long run to serve champagne and wine than to have an open bar with liquor. In recent years some excellent domestic and less expensive varieties of French champagne have found their way onto the American market, and a little experimenting on your part may uncover an excellent, dry champagne. While you don't want to insult your guests with a mediocre champagne, this isn't a wine tasting party either, so you can fudge a little on quality for the purpose of having some of the bubbly on hand for this special occasion. Sometimes, too, champagne is brought out for the toasts, and afterward everyone goes back to whatever they were drinking earlier.

In addition to champagne, you may serve wine, beer, or mixed drinks, and you should definitely have some soft drinks and bottled water on hand to offer to guests. Liquor comes in half-gallon, gallon, and five-gallon bottles, which are ideal for entertaining large groups, but for the purpose of determining how much liquor to order, we shall consider the quart bottle. You can count on getting sixteen 2-ounce servings from a quart of liquor. Allow half to one bottle of champagne or wine per person if those are the only beverages you are serving. It simply isn't gracious to run out, and there is no predicting how much people will drink at a reception. Unlike at a dinner party, you have no way to put a lid on the drinking—say, by announcing dinner. You will need almost one bottle of wine per person if you drink before and during dinner, less if you serve only appetizers. Roughly count on about four drinks per person and then order a few extra bottles just in case.

Remember that white wine and champagne must be chilled before serving, and that red wines must be opened an hour or so before serving to allow them to breathe.

While the popping of champagne corks is surely one of the pleasanter sounds in our cacophonous environment, be sure that the bottles are opened by someone who knows what he or she is doing. A flying champagne cork can be dangerous—and you don't want an accident to ruin your wedding day.

TOASTING THE BRIDE AND GROOM
The presence of newlyweds, alcoholic beverages, and guests creates a perfect occasion for toasts. Although

there is a rather rigid format for the toasting at a formal wedding, these formalities are often dispensed with when you are getting married again. Toasts, however, are an especially pleasant, warm way to wish a couple well, and they are usually led off by the best man or the father of either one of the couple. Actually, a toast may be offered by anyone, and the groom should certainly toast his bride. In these days of feminism, the bride may certainly toast her groom. Women can feel free to offer toasts these days. Toasts should be short and simple. Some sample toasts follow:

> "To John and Mary, may they always be as happy as they are today."
> "To John and Mary, all happiness."
> "To my wife (husband)."
> "To my new son-in-law (daughter-in-law)."
> Samuel Johnson offered an especially witty toast for this occasion: "Here's to a second marriage—the triumph of hope over experience."

When the toasting draws to an end, or threatens not to do so, signal the musicians to begin playing some fast, lighthearted piece.

And finally, there is the correct way of responding to a toast. You neither drink nor stand when you are being toasted. You simply smile and say or nod your thanks.

WORKING WITH THE CATERER

Perhaps the most complex aspect of planning the wedding is working with a caterer. And you will undoubtedly want to use a caterer for anything but the simplest of receptions. Food service, or even its supervision, is simply not something the bride should have to worry about. And if it's not your mother's party, then it's not fair to ask her to take on the task—after all, she is supposed to be a guest at this reception, and she may well have earned the honor if she organized and ran your first wedding for you.

Since supervision will be loose, you must choose a reliable caterer. Go to a caterer whose reputation is well known to you. Caterers offer a variety of services, so the first thing you need to find out is how wide a range of services the caterer you have chosen can provide.

Will he provide what is known as full catering, which should mean that he will supply all dishes, linens, serving dishes, and sometimes even sell you the beverages? Or will he provide semi- or half-catering, which can mean anything from bringing in the food and putting it in the oven for someone else to serve to preparing main dishes only. Be sure to ask whether or not he will serve the food, and if so, inquire about the number of persons who will be assigned to serving, what they will wear, and so on. In other words, you want to make sure that the persons serving will look and sound professional.

One way to save money on catering is to order only part of the meal. You might order the main dishes, for example, and make the appetizers yourself. If the caterer does not provide all the services you need, you may have to find a rental agency to supply what you lack. Party supply rental agencies, whose names can be obtained through personal recommendation or in the Yellow

Pages, can provide tables, chairs, silver and glassware, china, linens, and tubs to cool wine or champagne. They can be delivered the day before or the morning of the reception and they will be removed afterward.

Finally, whether you rent dishes from a caterer or an agency, figure out who can clean up the mess after the party. That's one thing you definitely won't want to be stuck with. Almost without exception, you do not clean up rental-agency supplies, but some caterers do not include cleaning up as part of their services, so be sure to ask.

The larger the caterer, the larger and wider the selection of food from which you can choose. Small caterers often have a few specialties, and while they may be willing to fill a particular request, you are probably safer letting them do what they know how to do best. Many large, established caterers do fairly traditional food or food that will appeal to the typical American palate, that is, rather bland. If you want to serve an authentic *ristaffel*, therefore, you would be better off hiring a couple of West Indians who know how to prepare this native dish rather than letting a caterer who does mostly American food attempt to reproduce it.

WORKING WITH THE BAKER

Wedding cakes are made by bakers; the caterer or restaurant with whom you deal probably won't supply your wedding cake, although they may be able to recommend someone.

Don't limit yourself to a traditional wedding cake unless you really want one. And if you do really want one, but don't think you are having enough guests to

justify a tiered cake, find a baker who will make a minia-
ture one—they are delightful. Aside from the fact that a
little bride and groom sitting atop your wedding cake
are not particularly appropriate this time, why limit
yourself to this kind of decoration, anyway? Consider
topping your cake with fresh flowers. A pastel wedding
cake is especially lovely. Consider a sheet cake with an
elaborate frosting display. You could also have some
other kind of dessert—a rich, luscious mousse or small
individual cakes.

WORKING WITH THE FLORIST

When you select your flowers, you will probably
want to order for your wedding and the reception at the
same time.

Flowers often are, but need not be, coordinated
with an overall color theme for the wedding. They can
look as if they belong at a wedding, or they can simply be
lovely floral arrangements that could appear anywhere
for any occasion.

One marvelous wedding took place in an apartment
furnished with sleek, modern furniture, of which black
was the predominant color. The only flowers were
numerous bouquets of calla lillies, which created a stunning effect, even if not exactly what one would expect to
find at a wedding.

Flowers are cheapest when you order them in season. In some seasons, though, that can limit your choice,
so you may want to combine a few expensive flowers
with some of the less costly, seasonal ones.

When you order flowers, consider where you are
being married and where the reception will be. A garden

wedding and reception, for example, cries out for garden flowers even if they don't come from the garden you
are using. Sophisticated flowers, as was the case with
the calla lillies, are most at home in sophisticated urban
houses or apartments.

Then, too, you can put to rest any notion of having
the traditional formal wedding arrangements that so
many florists suggest for first-time brides. Instead, you
may opt to fill baskets or even your own vases with floral
arrangements that will fill your home. At the table for a
sit-down meal, you may have individual vases at each
place setting rather than a centerpiece, or you may have
two or three small bouquets rather than one large one.
Consider using floral ropes to decorate the reception
area and even the altar if you are being married at home
or in a club or restaurant. They can be used to create
aisles, decorate hanging lamps or chandeliers, stair-
cases, and even a cloth backdrop. The possibilities for
what you can do with flowers, especially once you dis-
card the idea that your flowers must look as if they were
planned for a wedding instead of an elegant party, are
limited only by your and the florist's imaginations.

WORKING WITH THE PHOTOGRAPHER

Photographs are lovely mementoes, and you should
have as many made as you want to commemorate this
special day. What invariably happens at this wedding is
that the "formal" wedding portraits are taken right
along with the candids (and the kibitzers) at the reception. It is inappropriate to devote the attention to picture
taking as is done at a first wedding, but you won't want
to miss a chance to photograph close friends or relatives,

especially old ones, whom you may not see too often. Give the photographer directions on whom to include and point out the persons to him during the reception. Discuss with the photographer the degree of discretion you want him to use. He may not realize you have been through this before, and that you don't want to toss your bouquet or garter to the waiting crowds. Be sure he knows, so he won't start organizing any photos that you don't want taken. A list of suggestions for photos that you proabably will want for your wedding album appears in chapter 4.

Finally, if photos matter a lot to you, resist the urge to ask a friend and amateur photographer to take the pictures. Or if you do, ask more than one friend. That way, it won't be crucial if one person's photos don't turn out. And remember that friends who are asked to take photos (as compared with your Uncle Harry who never goes anywhere without a camera) are doing you a favor. They deserve, at minimum, a special dinner as a reward and a bottle of their favorite wine or brandy, or a book of photographs to add to their collection.

WORKING WITH THE MUSICIANS

There are several ways to have music at your wedding reception, and the only restriction on music is that it should match the degree of formality. If you have a formal dance reception, you will probably want to hire live musicians—the kind that can play dance music, which usually means a band.

You can also plan to use a stereo to supply the music or you can hire one or more musicians. Persons who enjoy classical music may want a string quartet to furnish background music; rock fans may want a rock band or combo. A pianist or violinist alone can make lovely reception music.

Talk with the musician about the kind of music you want and also be willing to listen to his or her suggestions. If you feel your wedding day won't be complete without a rendition of "Here Comes the Bride," then mention that to the musician. If, on the other hand, you don't want this vestige of blushing brides, then tell him that, too. If you want a song that has sentimental meaning for you and your new husband, then ask the musicians to play it. *And* if they are likely to play a song that meant something to you and your first husband simply because it is the kind of romantic song that is played at weddings, specify that you don't want to hear that song on this day.

Talk to the musicians about pacing the music. You will probably want something lively and cheerful when you arrive at the reception, and you will probably want something slower during dinner. Mention a signal or look that indicates that you want a different tempo of music—such as when you want to end the toasting or when you want guests to begin dancing. You can even ask the musicians to slow down the musical pace at about the time you hope your guests will begin to depart—and if you haven't paid for the musicians to play past a certain hour, they will probably slow things down considerably by packing up and going home.

Ask the musicians what their hourly fee is; that is usually how you will pay them, although you can try to negotiate for a flat fee. Ask how many breaks they take or discuss how many breaks you would like them to take or when you would like them to stop.

A NOTE OF COURTESY

Musicians and photographers work long, hard hours while everyone around them is having a good time. It is only courteous to offer them food and drinks of some sort while they take their breaks. You can, of course, suggest what they should drink and eat and where they should do it—they need not join your guests and you need not feel guilty about not asking them to do so.

TRADITIONS AND CUSTOMS

Finally, there are the customs and traditions that surround any wedding festivities. Some of these are dispensed with this time, and others are just too enjoyable to do without. Dancing, for instance. If you want to, you certainly should dance at your wedding reception. You need not be quite as rigid about the order of who dances with whom as you probably were if your first wedding was formal, but the bride does always dance the first dance with her new husband. She should also dance with her father and father-in-law and with the best man and any other male guests who ask her to dance. The groom, of course, dances with the mothers and with the bride's attendant.

Cutting the cake and toasting are small ceremonies that no one would want to do without. Throwing your floral bouquet and tossing your garter are two customs, along with throwing rice on the departing bridal couple, that you may want to avoid. And it probably won't even come up, but you have an absolute right not to drive away in a decorated car trailed by tin cans this time.

THE LENGTH OF THE RECEPTION

It's hard to control the length of the reception, except that most of your guests, in order to avoid being boors, will try to leave at an acceptable hour. Generally, a reception lasts four or five hours. The better the party, the longer persons stay. Since you are the host and hostess, you can't leave as you did when you had fewer responsibilities at your first weddings.

Generally, the time of day will dictate how long people will stay. If the reception is at 4 or 5 P.M., everyone should know that this is for cocktails and drinks and should leave by 9 or 10 P.M. An invitation for the hours from 11 A.M. to 2 P.M. is invariably for lunch only.

About the only serious problem you may have with those who linger is if you planned to go somewhere for dinner. If you have a reservation, you may just have to pass the word to latestayers that you will have to leave soon. There is no need to expand the party to include these persons. If you have planned a quiet dinner for two, you certainly won't want anyone along, and even if you have planned to dine with your attendants and your parents or some out-of-town friends, you still need not feel obligated to include anyone else.

THE LAST WORD

The best thing to keep in mind when planning this reception is that you are giving a party. Like any party, you will want it to be as smoothly planned as possible—and then on the day of the party, you will want to relax and enjoy yourself.

The next chapter contains menus and planning ideas for the various kinds of receptions: tea, cocktail party, stand-up buffet, sit-down buffet, formal dinner at home, formal dinner in restaurant, and dance.

Chapter Seven

WEDDING FESTIVITIES

*T**he* fact that this wedding reception should not be a duplicate of your first actually means that you have a great deal more freedom in planning it. You can have a real party this time, set any mood you like, declare a special theme, emphasize great food and drink, and plan stunning decorations. This chapter contains specific suggestions on how to plan each of several kinds of wedding receptions: an afternoon tea; a cocktail party; a stand-up buffet; a wedding breakfast; a sit-down buffet; a formal dinner; dinner in a restaurant, hall, or club; or an elegant supper dance. Menus are provided for each kind of reception, along with some menus designed for special themes, and some recipes for special punches. Recipes are not given for the foods described in the menus, but the foods are described in enough detail so that you can easily find recipes or describe what you want to a caterer.

AFTERNOON TEAS
The most popular reception is a tea, which follows a wedding held during the early afternoon. A tea is rela-

tively inexpensive, mainly because the food usually consists of small sandwiches and other delectable tidbits. You can serve a punch, have a mixed-drink bar, offer an assortment of wines, or serve the traditional wedding beverage—champagne.

Often, the foods for a tea are predictable and traditional: small sandwiches of tuna, turkey, or cucumber and cream cheese, and crabmeat-stuffed eggs are the perennial favorites. A champagne punch is the traditional beverage, and it is often accompanied by the Ginger Ale Punch recipe that appears at the end of this chapter.

While there is nothing wrong with this selection of food (and it is even looked forward to with great nostalgia by many persons), there are some variations to the traditional tea menu that you might want to consider using. You could, for example, serve a high tea, with either British or French accents. Instead of the traditional champagne or Ginger Ale Punch, you might serve a selection of unusual wines, Pimms cups, or sangria. Such teas are especially delightful for a spring or summer wedding. For fall or winter, you might choose a more filling tea menu—in which case a Russian tea table would offer an interesting and unusual variation.

RUSSIAN TEA TABLE

Caviar canapés
Buckwheat crepes with yogurt filling
Piroshky *with meat filling*
Smoked whitefish and salmon with onion and capers
Toast fingers and rolls

HIGH TEA WITH FRENCH ACCENT

Salted nuts
Canapés
Petits fours
Lemon-almond cookies
Individual chocolate mousses
Wedding cake

TRADITIONAL GARDEN TEA

Watercress and cucumber sandwiches
Minced chicken salad sandwiches
Minced ham sandwiches
Radish sandwiches with butter on rye bread
Cream cheese, smoked salmon, and dill on rye rounds
Liver pâté
Breads

COCKTAIL PARTIES

A cocktail party is actually nothing more than a slightly sophisticated version of a tea, made more sophisticated by the fact that alcoholic beverages are a large part of the entertainment. Best of all is to have a mixed-drink bar, but you can also limit the choice of beverages to wines, champagnes, or any combination thereof.

A cocktail party is appropriate following an afternoon wedding or one held around 5 or 6 P.M. The traditional hour for a cocktail party—6 P.M.—means that guests usually leave to go out to dinner, although some hangers-on may still be around at 10:30 or 11 P.M. A wedding celebration is especially likely to make the guests want to linger, so be prepared with lots of food and drink. Teas and cocktail parties are stand-up events. It is nice but not necessary to provide tables and chairs, and if you provide them, you still don't have to provide seating for each guest.

Cocktail party food is much like tea food, although some other foods are also served at cocktail parties. Strive for a balance between salty and nonsalty foods and hot and cold foods. If you want to add some weight to the menu, add a turkey or ham and possibly the trimmings for making sandwiches. For those who stay late, consider serving scrambled eggs and sausages as a light supper. Here is a list of foods that are suitable for cocktail parties:

Salted nuts

Raw vegetables (*crudites*) with a variety of dips

Individual quiches—onion, mushroom, tomato, eggplant, zucchini

Assortment of pâtés

Stuffed mushrooms

Sauteed vegetables with dips (use zucchini, carrots, onions)

Baked potato peelings roasted and served with dip

Eggs stuffed with variety of fillings

Individual ham and cheese sandwiches, hot or cold

Assortment of canapés

Cold shrimp with dips

Mushrooms remoulade

Vegetables *à la grecque*

Assortment of breads and crackers

Assortment of cheeses

If you would like to have a cocktail party with a theme, here is a suggested menu composed of Greek foods:

Hommus
Dolmas
Spanokapita
Eggplant dip and raw vegetables
Shrimp and feta cheese with vinaigrette dressing

STAND-UP BUFFETS

A stand-up buffet differs from a cocktail party in that it consists of a complete meal, albeit a meal that one can eat standing up or perched on the edge of a chair. Guests go up to a buffet table and fill their plates or are served food. (see illustrations of buffet tables). They usually eat informally at small tables or sitting at chairs. There is usually no bridal table at a stand-up buffet; the bride and groom mingle among their guests throughout the meal.

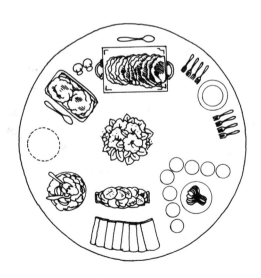

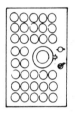
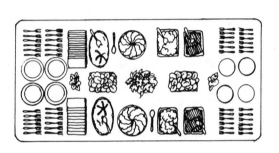
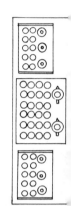
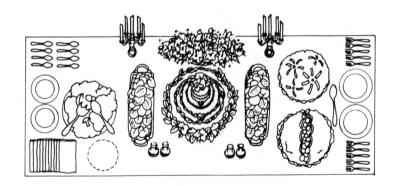

Food served at a stand-up buffet must be "fork" food, since juggling a knife and a fork is impossible. Consider serving a simple meal that consists of a hearty main dish, salad and cheese, and wedding cake. You can always plan a more complicated multicourse meal if you like. Guests might go up to the food table at first for hors d'oeuvres; later they might return for a first course, followed by the main dish and salad; and still later, wedding cake or your favorite dessert and coffee and tea could be served. Stand-up buffets are more successful, though, for both guests and host and hostess if they are kept fairly simple.

A meal should be served if the wedding is held in the evening, that is, during the dinner hour. Beverages can range from an open bar to wines and champagnes only. Especially if you are feeding a large crowd, there is no reason to serve after-dinner wines or brandies. Toasts are made before the meal or when the wedding cake is cut. Here are some menu suggestions for a stand-up buffet:

Crudites *with green mayonnaise dip*
Shrimp curry
Steamed rice
Mango chutney and lime pickle
Honeydew melon balls in champagne

Smoked salmon on toast fingers
Beef in aspic
Country pâté
Mushrooms in vinaigrette
Steak tartare
Assorted cheeses
Olives and pickles
Breads and crackers

SUMMER BUFFET

Seviche
Crab-stuffed cherry tomatoes
Deviled eggs
Duck liver pâté
Cold rice salad with capers and vegetables
Rolls

GREEK BUFFET

Pastitsio
Shredded carrot and zucchini with vinaigrette dressing
Feta cheese

INFORMAL BUFFET

Ham cornucopias stuffed with peas and corn
in homemade mayonnaise
Potato salad
Corn on the cob

PICNIC BUFFET

Crudites
Individual brioches filled with crab salad or with cream
cheese and smoked salmon or with chicken-chutney salad
Peach, cherry, and watermelon salad
served in scooped out watermelons

WEDDING BREAKFAST

When a wedding is held in the morning or early afternoon, a wedding breakfast, which is actually a lunch, is the traditional reception. With the recent trend toward brunches, though, some wedding breakfasts now actually feature breakfast or brunch food rather than lunch—take your choice. Such a menu is appropriate any time up to about 2 P.M., after which you probably want to choose a tea menu.

If the brunch is held before noon, you may serve only wines and champagne at the meal and skip offering mixed drinks. Here are some suggestions for wedding breakfasts, luncheons, and brunches:

GARDEN BREAKFAST

Melon with lime wedges
Crab and asparagus crepes
Fruit compote

BUFFET BREAKFAST

Platters of smoked fish, garnished with
onion, lemon, and capers
Homemade applesauce
Selection of hot breads and sweet rolls

THREE TYPES OF FORMAL LUNCHEON

Cheese soufflé
Rack of lamb with bearnaise
Rice
Green salad and cheeses
Bread

Asparagus vinaigrette
Lobster mousse
Carrots vichy
Rolls

Watercress soup, chilled
Sautéed pork medallions
Potatoes Anna
Green salad and cheeses
Rolls

SIT-DOWN BUFFET

More elaborate than a stand-up buffet is a sit-down buffet, where guests take or are served the food and then sit down at a table or tables to eat. Numerous small tables can be placed around the room or garden or, if the group is small enough, everyone can be seated at one table. Tablecloths, cloth napkins, and flowers are especially nice touches at a formal meal. Flatware and napkins can be at each place, or guests can pick them up as they are served. Name cards are appropriate but not necessary at this kind of reception. If everyone sits together, the bride and groom should be accorded positions of honor. At a U-shaped table, they might sit as noted in the illustration that follows:

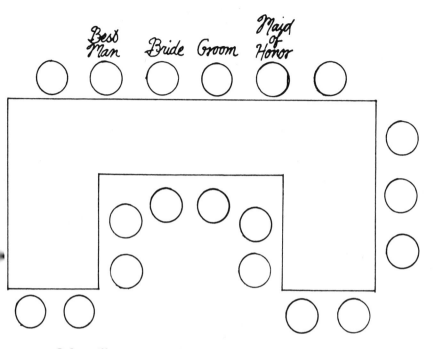

Other illustrations later in the chapter show alternate seating arrangements.

The choice of food is almost limitless at a sit-down buffet. You can have an ultraformal menu, fork food as for a stand-up buffet, or casual food. Usually, though, the meal is not served in more than one or two courses to avoid having the guests spend most of their time going to and from the food table. When the bride and groom cut the cake, it is often served to the seated guests. A flamed food or any other showy dish is usually not served at a buffet of any sort, since all the guests do not go through the food line at the same time and not everyone would be able to observe the display of the food before the servers started serving it. Here are some menus for a sit-down buffet:

SUMMER BUFFET DINNER

Quiche Lorraine
Turkey breast tonnato
Grilled cold tomatoes
Cold rice salad
Cheese and bread

FOUR TYPES OF ELEGANT BUFFET DINNER

Fish quenelles with hollandaise sauce
Rice pilaf
Grilled tomatoes
Cheese
Salad
Bread

Crudites
Crab quiche
Blanquette of veal
Marinated string beans

Carbonnades flamandes *(Flemish beef stew*
made with beer or ale)
Rice
Salad and cheese

Chicken sautéed with vegetables
Cucumber mousse
Steamed rice
Salad
Cheeses

FORMAL DINNER

A formal dinner is the most elegant small reception you can possibly have. It is difficult and expensive to serve more than twenty or thirty—and many persons draw the line at ten or twelve—at this kind of party, but if you want a very special, small and lovely reception, this is the reception for you.

A formal dinner calls for formal clothes, although you can actually wear anything from suits and dressy clothes to evening dresses and black tie. If you have never entertained so formally, this is the perfect time to start. Send printed, handwritten, or partially printed and partially handwritten invitations to your guests. Be sure to indicate the day, hour, and dress, as well as to ask for a response. Then carry out the dinner as elegantly as you can.

Often, you may be married earlier in the day or even a day or so before the day of the dinner, but the dinner is still your official reception. The dinner should be set no earlier than 7 P.M., and preferably it should be scheduled for 8 or 9 P.M.

A formal dinner calls for place cards, and the bride and groom sit together rather than apart as they would at any other type of dinner party. Two possible ways to arrange the seating are shown on the following page:

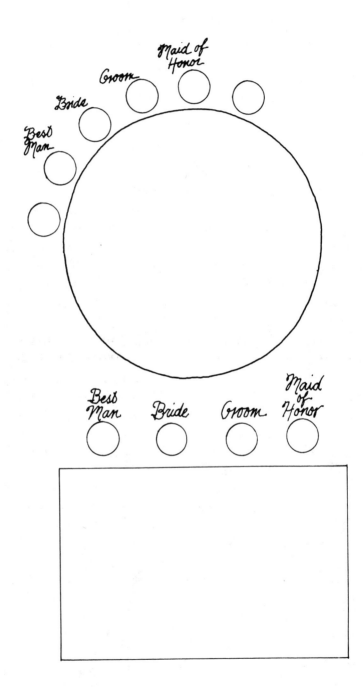

Wines should accompany the meal, with light wines preceding heavy ones and white ones coming before red ones. Champagne may be served with appetizers or with the dessert, which can be wedding cake or any other dessert you choose to serve. Remember that few caterers will be prepared to bake a wedding cake, so this will probably have to be ordered elsewhere, although you can expect the caterer to help you serve it. The traditional wedding cake cutting ceremony is appropriate at a formal dinner.

The food for a formal dinner is always special and elegant, although it need not be fussy. It should be presented in courses: the first course consists of appetizers or soup (or you can serve both in two courses); this is followed by a meat course, a salad, and dessert. A more elaborate formal dinner might be expanded to include appetizer, soup, fish course, meat course, salad and cheeses, and dessert. You can also skip the soup and serve the entree, salad and cheeses, and dessert, but if you do this, a nice touch is to serve a small appetizer with predinner drinks. Any general etiquette book will supply all the details on serving these courses and on setting the table for a formal dinner.

If the caterer is skilled enough, by all means let him show off his specialty—a perfect roast, fish *en croute*, or whatever he does well. All the food should be prepared from scratch; frozen and convenience foods are not acceptable at a formal dinner. At such a dinner, the food is, if not the main event, an important part of the evening.

Neither the host or hostess nor the guests participate in the food service. If possible, hire a caterer who can do everything from preparing to serving the food, and if you can really splurge, hire a maid to take guest's coats and a butler or bartender. The bride and groom cut the wedding cake themselves, although the waiters or waitresses usually serve it.

The table should be set with your very best china and silver, a white or pastel cloth, and matching napkins. If you don't have nice serving pieces, rent them for the occasion. You can use a floral centerpiece, several small bouquets, or flowers at each place, but do have fresh flowers and lighted candles on the table. Since you will be toasting and talking with everyone at the table, as opposed to other formal dinners where persons sometimes talk only to their right and left-hand dinner partners, be sure the centerpiece and candles are low enough not to intrude.

Here are some menus for a formal sit-down dinner:

Assortment of canapés
Whitefish rolled and stuffed with grapes
and seasoned breadcrumbs
Roast duck in orange sauce
Peas and rice
Salad and cheese

Baked mixed seafood
Leg of lamb
Fresh broccoli soufflé
Potatoes and carrots as garnish
Salad and cheese

Cream of carrot soup
Escargot

Stuffed baked breast of capon
Wild rice
Asparagus with hollandaise
Salad and cheese

Cold cucumber soup
Baked red snapper
Roast saddle of venison
Pureed vegetables (turnips and peas)
Braised endive
Salad and cheeses

Oysters Rockefeller
Trout Amandine
Curried rice
Steamed broccoli
Salad and cheese

Cold broccoli soup
Ham in pastry crust
Puree of celeriac
Steamed rice
Salad and cheese

Seafood bisque
Tournedos with bearnaise sauce and vegetable garnish
Sautéed new potatoes
Salad and cheese

SUPPER DANCE

The most elaborate celebration and the best way to handle a crowd is to plan a supper dance. If done right, though, a supper dance is a fairly expensive proposition. It calls for live music and a supper served late in the evening, around eleven or twelve o'clock. Cocktail foods are offered along with drinks throughout the evening. Guests can sit down to eat if there is room, or the meal can be a stand-up buffet.

A formal supper dance is usually an elegant affair but you can plan any kind of dance that suits you. You can have guests wear black tie or jeans, and they can dance to a swing orchestra or to contemporary band music.

A supper dance usually begins around 9 P.M. Because of the hour, you may have gotten married earlier in the day, or even a day or two before; this doesn't prevent the supper dance from being your official wedding reception.

At a supper dance, you may dance until the wee hours, but because some guests may have to leave before the bride and groom do, be sure to cut the wedding cake as soon as everyone finishes dinner, so that those guests who have to leave can do so.

Here are some menus for a supper dance:

Mixed salted nuts
Vegetables à la grecque
Smoked turkey
Rare roast beef in paper thin slices
Pumpernickel
Asparagus mousse

Shrimp and cream cheese ball
Assorted cheeses
Creamed asparagus and eggs in bechamel sauce

Roulades with spinach and mushroom filling
Ratatouille
Fruit salad

Antipasto
Lasagne
Green salad
Italian cheeses and breads

Duck liver pâté
Ham mousse
Stuffed eggs
Assorted cheeses and breads

Scrambled eggs
Curried veal kidneys
Sautéed green tomatoes
Cheeses and breads

MENUS WITH A THEME

Here are several menu ideas based on special cuisines or themes:

INFORMAL NEW ORLEANS BUFFET DINNER

Oyster and sausage jambalaya
Green tossed salad
Cheeses and breads

SOUTHERN STYLE SIT-DOWN BREAKFAST

Scrambled eggs
Glazed Virginia cured ham
Spoon bread
Relish trays
Hot rolls

SAN FRANCISCO BUFFET

Cioppino
Hot Italian bread
Tossed green salad

FRENCH COUNTRY DINNER

Choucroute garni
Green beans vinaigrette
Italian bread

ELEGANT STAND-UP BUFFET

Raw vegetables with dips
Chicken liver and mushroom strudel
Stuffed celery and mushrooms
Assortment of cheeses and breads

OUTDOOR BARBEQUE

Split barbequed Cornish hens
Corn on the cob
Tossed salad

ELEGANT PICNIC

Bite-sized mushroom and/or cheese quiches
Pâté of duck liver
Cold zucchini stuffed with ham salad
made with homemade mayonnaise
Cheeses
Green tossed salad

WEDDING PUNCHES

Here is an assortment of usual and unusual punches
and beverages suitable for serving at a wedding:

CHAMPAGNE PUNCH

The traditional wedding punch.

1 orange
3 lumps sugar
3 dashes bitters
½ cup cognac
4 bottles champagne

Peel orange, taking care not to remove white pith,
which is bitter. Use peels and save rest of orange for
some other use. Mix all the ingredients together
and serve well chilled. Approximately twenty
servings.

TEA PUNCH

Another old favorite for weddings.

2 quarts strong tea
2 cups Grand Marnier or Cointreau
2 quarts dark rum
2 quarts bourbon
2 cups orange juice

4 bottles champagne
Sugar to taste

Mix all ingredients together and chill. 100 servings.

CASSIS PUNCH

6 bottles dry white wine
1¼ cups creme de cassis
15 orange slices, halved
2 cups strawberries

Blend liquids; float fruits on top. 40 servings.

SANGRIA

8 oranges
4 lemons
8 cloves
2 cups confectioners' sugar
8 quarts good red wine
Fresh mint sprigs

Peel fruit and cut into thin slices. Put in punch
bowl, add cloves and sugar. Pour in wine. Chill.
Add mint about an hour before serving. 20 to 25
servings.

WHITE WINE WITH ORANGE ESSENCE

This recipe must be started about a month before
you plan to use it.

24 oranges
6 cloves
3 sticks cinnamon
3 quarts dry white wine
Sugar to taste
12 tablespoons cognac

Remove peels from oranges and let them dry in a cool place for two weeks. Save orange for other use. Put dried orange in container that has a top; add cloves and cinnamon. Pour in wine, cover, and put in dark, cool place for eight to ten days. (If you must use your refrigerator, store in least cold area.) Strain the wine. Pour three cups into enamel saucepan; add sugar to taste, and cook over low heat just until sugar is dissolved. Return wine to container, add cognac, and stir. Serve ice cold with orange twist. 10 servings.

NONALCOHOLIC PUNCH

Another traditional wedding punch.

4 quarts ginger ale
1 quart fruit flavored sherbet
Fruits for garnish

Blend all ingredients together. Serve chilled. 30 to 35 servings.

A RESTAURANT RECEPTION

Many couples today plan a reception in a favorite restaurant. Usually it has sentimental meaning for them, and they can't imagine gathering anywhere else for this special occasion. Restaurants are limited in the numbers they can accommodate, and you should, if at all possible, try to obtain a private room. With privacy, you can indulge in as much revelry as you like without bothering other diners and without feeling constrained by them. If you can't obtain a private room, and you still have the reception in a restaurant, you must act with some restraint. Don't stand for toasts and don't be so noisy that you ruin the dinners of others in the restaurant.

Two items must be ordered individually and brought to the restaurant: the centerpiece or floral arrangements and the wedding cake. Simply ask the restaurant what arrangements you can make for the delivery of both on the day of the reception.

In choosing restaurant food, you are usually limited to the menu, plus whatever special dishes the chef may have in his repertoire. Ask about any special foods you may want, but don't expect a Chinese chef to turn out a French meal or vice versa. You do make the decisions about what is served to everyone rather than passing around menus to all your guests; it's a way of keeping the cost down, among other things.

Try to have everyone arrive at the same time so you can all be seated at once. You might ask a friend to check in with the restaurant in the early afternoon (or you could do this yourself) to make sure that everything is in order, that the cake has arrived, that the flowers are in place, that there are enough chairs, that the delectable mousse is being prepared as ordered.

When you plan the menu, also discuss the beverages with the chef or wine steward. You will undoubtedly want to buy by the bottle. The restaurant should take back any unopened bottles, as should any good wine dealer. If the restaurant does not insist that you buy from them, shop around to get the best price on beverages. Champagne and wines are excellent choices for this type of reception, and you may also want the waiter to take orders for a round or two of mixed drinks when everyone arrives.

At most restaurant receptions, the group is small enough to be seated at one table, even if the table must be arranged into a U-shape or some other shape to accommodate everyone. The bride and groom are obviously the center of attention. You may want to arrange place cards for the other guests, an especially tactful gesture since the guests may not know each other and you are likely to know who will probably get along with whom.

Tipping after such a celebration runs along the same lines as it does in any fine restaurant. The average tip is 20 percent, with 15 percent going to the waiter and 5 percent to the captain. If there is no captain, you may want to tip the waiter a little more. The headwaiter is tipped for special services, and since he may help you plan the reception as well as make sure that it runs smoothly, he should be tipped in the range of 5 to 10 percent. Coat checkers, doormen, and restroom attendants are tipped by the guests who use these services.

Wedding receptions held in clubs or halls are usually organized in much the same way as a restaurant reception. You must talk with the food service person to determine what will be served, and you probably will have to supply your own cake and flowers. The choice of food may also be more limited in these places.

One enterprising couple I know rented a suite in their favorite hotel, held the wedding reception there, and then used the suite for a marvelous honeymoon weekend. They obtained a weekend rate on the suite, which is now offered by many hotels, and they took advantage of all the hotel's services in planning their reception.

OTHER ENTERTAINMENTS

While it is not appropriate for you to have showers and other similar entertainments for this wedding, nor will you be likely to have the traditional rehearsal dinner or the bridesmaid's luncheon or bachelor dinner, there will still be a lot of prewedding festivities. You may want to have an engagement party to announce your plans to marry, and you can also entertain your maid of honor and best man at some point before or shortly after the wedding. An especially nice gesture is to ask your attendants to be your first dinner guests in your new home together. You may also feel that you want to entertain out-of-town guests who arrive before the wedding or stay over the next day.

ENTERTAINING OUT-OF-TOWN GUESTS

You are, strictly speaking, under no obligation to entertain out-of-town guests, but since this wedding will undoubtedly be a small gathering of your closest friends, presumably anyone coming from far away is a good friend who deserves some special attention, if you can possibly find the time and means to give it. Often, these days, out-of-town guests are invited to the rehearsal dinner, but since you will not be having one, why not plan a dinner anyway for out-of-town guests and anyone else whom you want to see? You might even plan a barbeque or some other casual meal. Or you might schedule a brunch or luncheon the day after the wedding and reception, which is the time that out-of-town guests most often find themselves at loose ends. The parents of the bride and groom often entertain their relatives and friends at parties like this these days, and if you are giving your own wedding and aren't taking off on a wedding trip right away, such a party might be a lot of fun. And if you are leaving right away on a wedding trip, it might be a good idea to pass this along to your out-of-town guests so they can make their own plans.

AN ENGAGEMENT PARTY

You can give your own engagement party, or you can let your family or a close friend give it for you. The traditional way of announcing an engagement is simply to send invitations to a party "in honor of" the about-to-be-engaged couple. Everyone who knows the couple will get the message that an official announcement is pending, and if there are any doubts, they are cleared up when the toasting begins.

Invitations should not mention directly that this is an engagement party. To do so obligates guests to bring gifts, and that is the last thing you want to do.

An engagement can be announced at a small, intimate dinner or at a large cocktail party or at anything in between. Keep the size of your wedding in mind, though, when planning the size of the engagement party. If you are having a very private, small wedding, then a large engagement party should not hurt anyone's feelings if they aren't asked to the wedding and reception. If, however, you are planning a wedding for, say, fifty, with a reception for the same number, then it is not polite to invite one hundred persons to an engagement party. In fact, you risk offending about fifty of your friends.

WHEN FRIENDS OFFER TO GIVE SHOWERS

A well-meaning friend may offer to give a shower for you, thus shifting the final decision to you. Resist the urge to accept and turn your friend down graciously, or suggest a nontraditional party that in no way smacks of a shower. Even if your first wedding was hundreds of miles away and you have an entirely new set of friends now, many persons will know that you were married before, and it simply is not appropriate to go through the same set of prewedding festivities twice.

If friends do plan a shower for you without your knowledge, there is little you can do but be gracious about the whole thing. In addition to writing thank-you notes, you should also try to entertain, either separately or as a group, the persons who entertained you so graciously.

Good parties to celebrate remarriages include wine tastings, cookouts and barbeques, formal and informal dinners—anything that skips the many rituals, including gift giving, that surround traditional showers. Most parties are coed.

Chapter Eight

WORKING OUT
RELATIONSHIPS

*G*etting married is a scary enough experience for most persons. And unlike most other things in life, it doesn't get any easier the next time you do it. Also, it's not exactly something that one plans to do very many times in one's life. But here you are doing it again—and you're more excited and happier than you ever thought you would be. So what is that little gnawing sensation that hits your stomach every so often?

It is more than likely anxiety and tension. After all, you *have* done this before. Even if you are madly in love, you still are probably not quite as starry-eyed this time around. Maturity has a way of doing that to you, making you put things just a little bit more into perspective.

If you read the books and articles on getting married the first time, you probably already know that one of the major purposes—in theory, anyway—of the engagement period is to work out any differences you may have and to find a way to merge your two personalities and styles. Most couples make only feeble attempts to do this the first time around. They may discuss the pros and cons of a queen- versus a king-sized bed or how to spend the big check they were given, but that's about as far as most couples get.

This time around, though, you may find yourself far more inclined to talk about your future lives together, and in more realistic terms. Furthermore, you may even find that you *need* to talk. Don't be surprised if a few ghosts from the past show up to haunt you during this period of your life. This is only to be expected. And remember that in addition to everything else that is going on emotionally, you may also be merging households, careers, children, and long-established sets of friends, all of which can add to the tension. It helps, too, to recognize that you are a little older now and perhaps less flexible than when you were first a blushing bride—all this merging and shifting may take a little more thought and planning and discussion than you ever imagined.

As for the ghosts that may suddenly appear, they have a purpose, and talking about them is one way to exorcise them. Whether you have had five weeks or five years between marriages, it is a pretty safe guess that you haven't worked out and put to rest every single hurt and frustration that you suffered. If you don't think and talk about your past mistakes, you're liable to make the same mistakes all over again, so don't be afraid to air your feelings on what may seem to be touchy subjects. Obviously, your husband-to-be doesn't want to hear what a wonderful amateur carpenter your ex-husband was any more than you want to hear that his ex-wife was a great gourmet cook. The things you have to work out go deeper than that.

One woman I know, who had resented all the Sunday evenings that she felt obligated to spend with her ex-mother-in-law, always picked a fight with her fiance just before they were scheduled to visit his parents. Sometimes she would get so angry that she would refuse to go to dinner with him. One night, she went even farther, becoming angry over a dinner conversation with him at his parent's house and storming out. Fortunately, when he returned home later that night, she was able to talk about her feelings and to admit that she was playing out an old animosity she felt toward her ex-mother-in-law. She said she liked his parents and wanted to see them, but she also wanted to avoid the feeling that she had to see them on a regular basis, such as every Tuesday or even every week. They worked out a compromise in which she felt free not to accompany him on every visit to his parents' home. Without this conversation, though, her fiance would have had no idea what was bothering her.

Once you have made the decision to marry again, you may well find old feelings creeping in to blur your euphoria. Rather than hiding the feelings, though, you need to let them out, discuss the old wounds, and then talk about ways to build your new life together.

BUILDING YOUR RELATIONSHIP

Since getting married again will undoubtedly bring up feelings about that other marriage, you may as well discuss the past—to some degree.

If you are still smarting because your first husband took a vacation without you, for example, and you never understood why he did that, and you would be upset if this husband did it, then you probably need to talk about it. If you felt that your first husband never really let you be independent, and independence was—and is—very important to you, then you need to discuss your feelings about independence. It's far better to let out these old feelings now than to release them in the tension of your first big postmarital fight.

Once you have aired your feelings about the past, it's time to look to the future. A psychologist who has counseled many couples before marriage said she always tells her clients they must discuss three things before they marry: how they plan to spend and share their money, how they plan to share housekeeping chores, and how they feel about having children. If you are chuckling and saying to yourself, "But who wouldn't discuss such important things?" then you may also be surprised to know that most of her patients who return for more counseling after they have married do so because they have failed to work out one of these three areas.

WORKING OUT FINANCES

Money is always hard to talk about, and it may be a particularly painful subject for divorced persons who may have had a few hard lessons over finances when their first marriages broke up. A woman may have resented not receiving financial support to get back on her feet if she didn't work during her first marriage. Her standard of living may have changed when she began to live on her income alone. A man may be paying child support or alimony that takes a sizeable chunk out of his paycheck every week. Money is also a major source of tension in a marriage, so you may as well talk about these things now and reach some agreements about it.

You also need to talk about how you will spend your money. Discuss whether or not you want joint bank accounts, separate accounts, or a combination thereof. Do you want to set up any special savings accounts? Decide what important things you will save for. One couple I knew who were poor communicators agreed to open a joint bank account to save money, even though they had not really clarified which of their goals was more important to them. When there was enough money to discuss spending, she thought they were going to use it to have a baby, and he thought they were going to buy a new car with it.

You may also have to make some changes in your financial arrangements. Do you need to change a will? Declare new beneficiaries on insurance policies? Buy a homeowner's policy or an apartment renter's policy? A working woman may, for the first time, think about taking life insurance, particularly if she and her husband will be planning to depend upon her income. Is the auto insurance in both your names? Does one of you have a comprehensive enough health insurance policy so that you can use that alone, or do you need both your policies?

If you are a two-paycheck couple, you may be looking for a way to allot your salaries fairly, especially if one person earns substantially more than the other. One marriage counselor we talked with reported his method, which he has shared with many persons over the years. He suggests that each person contribute to household expenses based on a ratio of his earnings. That means that if one of you earns $40,000 a year as a stockbroker and the other earns $20,000 as a fledgling lawyer, then the $40,000-a-year wage earner contributes double what the $20,000-a-year earner contributes to household expenses. Also, of course, if one of you pays alimony or child support, you may want to take that into account. The money that is left over is each person's private spending money.

Most of the couples I talked with said that they were far less willing to merge funds entirely this time, not because they didn't have confidence in their new spouses, but because each person had become used to running his own finances. So even if you handled money in a rather traditional way the first time you were married, be prepared to be more flexible this time around. You will probably find that it suits you better than the old way.

SHARING HOUSEHOLD CHORES

How you share household chores is another important subject to discuss before you marry. If one of you doesn't work and the other does, the bulk of the housekeeping may fall on the shoulders of the person who doesn't work. If you both work, you need to find a way to share housekeeping tasks. Again, don't get caught up in setting up a rigid schedule. You're both likely to be happier if you leave a lot of room for compromise in this area. If you absolutely hate doing laundry, and he actually likes doing it, for example, then offer to do something he finds really distasteful in exchange for his doing the laundry. Some couples work out an alternating schedule: one cooks one week while the other is responsible for cleaning, and then they swap chores the following week. There is no one right way to work out this aspect of your lives—you do what works for you—but your marriage will be better if you enter it having this vital area pretty much ironed out.

TALKING ABOUT CHILDREN

The third and final area that ought to be discussed before you marry is whether or not you want children. Almost everyone who has been married previously has some feelings about children, and persons who already have children often have very definite feelings. Those feelings probably won't lessen with time or marriage, so if you desperately want children, and the man you are marrying doesn't, then however painful the topic is, you are better off discussing it now—before you leap into marriage.

Finally, it helps to talk about the kind of marriage you want, what your hopes and expectations are for this marriage.

PRESERVING YOUR SPACE

While you are working to iron out your lives together, you may also find that you have some feelings about preserving your own space—the part of you that struggled to find an apartment at the bottom of the apartment market when your ex-spouse had left you with $800 and the dog; the part that paid off a large settlement to your ex-spouse and then worked hard to build up a savings account to replenish it; the part of you that has decided, somewhat peevishly, that you really must have your own Sunday newspaper, one that you don't have to share with anyone else. Do you want to take separate vacations? Do you want to be free to go elsewhere when his children visit one weekend a month? Do you, as a working woman, feel that you want to keep your professional name? Almost none of these things become big problems if they are talked about now, and any of them is likely to flare up as larger than it actually is if you don't sit down for a few long, honest discussions now.

CHANGING NAMES—YOURS AND YOUR CHILDREN'S

Most women have definite ideas about whether or not they want to assume the use of their new husband's surname—and increasingly the answer is no. Women who have been divorced and who gave up their father's name when they married the first time are continuing to use their first husband's surname even after they re-marry. Often it is the name under which they established themselves professionally and, if they have children, it provides an added form of identity for the children. Persons whom you meet in adult life rarely know whether your last name is your father's surname or your first husband's surname anyway. Other women resume the use of their maiden names, while some never gave it up.

Another issue is the names of your children. Their names do not change simply because you marry someone and you and your children begin living with him. Unless your new husband adopts your children by a previous marriage, their legal names remain the same as that of their natural father.

If you do change your name, be sure to change it on

the myriad documents in your life—social security insurance and work forms, passport, wills, and any magazines and newspapers you subscribe to, along wtih any credit cards.

COPING WITH YOUR INLAWS
AND FAMILIES

Although it happens rarely today, you may find yourself with a set of inlaws who thought marriage was forever and who aren't willing to accept you readily only because you are The Second Wife. There is little you can do about this situation, except be polite and patient, and hope that time will soften your new family, as it invariably does.

Then, too, you may find yourself with a similar parent problem. Comparisons with ex-spouses are inevitable, and you may find yourself defending or making excuses for ways that your new partner differs from your ex-husband. This is one of those times in your life when you have to trust your own judgment. You know why things didn't work out in your previous marriage, and you know what has caused you to choose someone fairly different to marry this time, but your parents may not understand this. Without divulging more about your personal life than you are willing to share with your parents, explain your actions. Whatever you do, though, remember that your support and loyalty should be with your new husband. After all, you would expect the same thing from him in dealing with his family.

BECOMING A STEPMOTHER

Becoming a parent overnight is one of the hardest things you will ever do. You shouldn't do it without giving a great deal of thought and energy to planning how you will handle this major change in your life.

For starters, if you do not know a lot about children, begin by reading about them. A school librarian or your local librarian—or even the children's teachers—can suggest books that will help you learn more about children and how they think and act.

You also need to develop an understanding of your husband's relationship and responsibilities toward his children. They are part of his life now, and they will always be part of his life, even after he has ended his official responsibilities to them. He loves all of you, and it is not fair to ask or expect him to decide which of you he loves more.

As for some of the more practical aspects of becoming an instant parent, try to arrange for an easy transition once you are married. Spend time getting to know the children individually. Watch them with their father so you can observe how that relationship works. Plan your new life carefully. Especially if you work, you will probably need some extra household help—perhaps a cleaning woman or a teenage girl to sit with the children between the time that they get home from school and when you get home from work. You will also need babysitters, if the children are too young to stay home alone, for those nights when you and your husband will want to go out alone. Line these up far in advance.

Don't wait until the first week of married—and family—life to take care of these details. Having everything ready to fall into place before you all start living together will make everything easier on everyone.

Make the kids a part of your lives from the start.

Invite them to go to an occasional movie with you, and plan some family outings together. Also remember to reserve some time to yourselves, just as regular parents do. You do not need to overdo the mothering to the point of personal sacrifice. In fact, you are wise to realize that you will function better as the kids' friend than as their mother. Presumably, they have a mother, and they do not need another one; they may, in fact, resent your trying to assume that role.

Make firm rules and assign chores to the children from the start. Remember that this is your house, too. Most kids are smart enough to complain that they don't have to work at their mother's house—which may or may not be true, but is still irrelevant. Just tell them that's fine, but this house belongs to all of you, and they are expected to contribute as full family members. They may grumble a bit, but in the long run, you will have earned their respect and preserved your sanity.

Do try to get to know each child individually, to become a special friend who is responsive to the child's needs. Plan some special time alone with each child so you can get to know each other better.

WEEKEND STEPMOTHERING

This tour of duty differs from being a full-time mother. When the children are only around on weekends, or for a few short weeks, you may find yourself overdoing the affection and gift-giving. In part, this is a way of trying to win their love, and most kids are savvy enough to know this *and* to use it to their full advantage. It also won't win you any true affection. Then, too, if a child feels any shyness or resentment over your presence, he or she may find it hard to accept your generosity, regardless of the form it takes. Remember that giving excessive amounts of affection is also a way of demanding affection, something that children may pick up on, even if they aren't able to understand it. Just stay calm and act like yourself. Don't demand kisses and hugs that aren't willingly given.

Do establish some rules, and then stick to them. This is as much for your sake as for the sake of the children. Many new stepmothers are too anxious to please their stepchildren as a way of pleasing a new husband, and the next thing they know, the children are running the whole show. Do you think the children should make their own beds? Keep their living space or bedrooms clean? Do the dishes? Don't be afraid to ask, and do be consistent about whatever chores you expect them to do.

Present a united front with your husband about what is expected of them when they visit your home. You should both agree to and insist that the rules be followed. Children are quite adept at spotting a chink in the armor, and are excellent at taking advantage of it.

Try not to argue when the children are around. If they lived with you all the time, it would be only natural for them to witness arguments, but when they are there for so short a time, they should be spared fights, especially fights that may relate to them. If you want to discuss some aspect of their visit, do it after they have left or before they arrive.

In an almost opposite vein, don't criticize their father to them. It's only confusing, and they probably heard enough of that sort of thing when their mother and father were in the process of breaking up. Do maintain a sense of humor. So you haven't been able to call home all afternoon because little Henry cut the telephone wires while he was playing espionage games with his friends—it's not the end of the world, and it may even have its funny side if you think about it long enough. Children are funny, and they do have a great sense of humor at a very young age. It helps to learn to appreciate this side of them.

Do let the children have time alone with their father. They may already worry that you have usurped some of the affection they formerly held when you became a part of their father's life, and one way you can help to show them that they matter as much as ever to him is to allow them some time alone with him. Go spend an afternoon with a friend you haven't seen for awhile. Go to a movie. You don't have to make yourself scarce for long; a few hours will do.

As you get to know your stepchildren, you will undoubtedly work out your own way of relating to them. As a final note, if the man you are marrying is the person who is about to undergo instant parenthood, show him these hints. They work equally well for step-fathers.

RELATING TO YOUR OWN CHILDREN

If you are like most mothers, your relationship to your children probably shifted when you started to date. Prepare yourself for another shift if you announce plans to marry. What follows are some hints for coping with the situation.

Don't announce plans to marry out of the blue. Help

prepare your kids by letting them know that this man is special and by saying that you are thinking about marriage. Then when you do make a decision, tell your children first. How you tell them may have more to do with each child, how they felt about the divorce, and how they are liable to feel about your marrying again. Older children obviously have a much rougher time with this than younger ones do, but younger children may not know how to show you that they are upset or may not be able to tell you exactly what it is they are upset about. If your children are well adjusted and are tuned in to the fact that you are about to remarry, you may be able to announce your plans casually over dinner. If there is likely to be some backlash, especially from one child, you may want to talk to each child alone.

Give your children a chance to get to know their stepfather, but don't push anything or, by words or actions, demand that they love him. They will when they are ready.

Let your kids participate in the wedding if they want to, but be sensitive to the fact that a child also may *not* want to do this. A child who was particularly upset by a divorce, and who may still have mixed loyalties toward his parents, may not feel good about standing up at your wedding to someone else. Be prepared to accept this and more: the child may not even feel comfortable attending the wedding, and he or she should not be pressured to do so.

Try to spend some regular amounts of time alone with your children during the engagement period so they won't feel abandoned or unloved.

Talk to the children about their new life, especially

if they will be making any major changes, such as moving into a new house or apartment or going to a new school. Let them participate in this planning as much as you possibly can. Give them room to vent any anxieties they may be feeling about a change in their lives. Moving can be just as anxiety provoking to a child as to an adult.

If you are a widow and about to remarry, talk with your children about their father, your feelings for him, and your feelings for the man you are about to marry. If you remove their father's picture from your room or some part of the house in deference to your husband-to-be, explain the gesture to the children, and put the picture in their room. This might also be a nice time to give the children some special memento related to their father that you have been saving—letters, a war medal, or some favorite possession of his.

Children don't always understand that love is an expandable emotion, and they may experience some trepidation about whether or not you still love them when you remarry. The best way to be sure that they know you do is to tell them.

CHILDREN—MERGING HIS AND YOURS

After becoming an instant parent, the next biggest step is merging your kids and his into one happy family. Whatever you do, try not to play favorites. This is, unfortunately, easier said than done. Before you blame his children for a fight that all your children were involved in, remember that they are his children. Try to sort out what is truly fair to all the children.

Whether in anger or pride, never say, "You won't

believe what your son did today" or anything to that effect. If Susy or Billy brought home good grades, make sure that they know how pleased the family is. Say, "Did you see Susy's report card? Isn't that just wonderful that she got such good grades?"

Finally, treat each child as an individual and get to know each child. It may be easy to spend time with your children alone, but also try to spend some time with your stepchildren. You are forming one family unit, and the best way to strengthen its ties is to show that you feel you are all in this together.

Chapter Nine

⤳

YOUR PLACE OR HIS—SETTING UP HOUSEKEEPING

Possibly the most trying part of remarrying—but also sometimes the best part—is working out your living arrangements. For one thing, this time you aren't going from living in a college dorm or with room-mates to running your first home. Most likely, you have both been living in and running your own households. You may both have furniture left over from your previous marriages, to say nothing of a lot of wedding gifts that you're probably eating and drinking from, and you probably are unsure what to do about these gifts when you start living with your new husband. Or you may have been living an unsettled life, but you now feel the need to settle down in a real home with real furniture, a well-stocked kitchen, and a well-stocked linen closet. Or maybe you are both settled in where you are, and your marriage means that you will tear up your households and merge into one.

Regardless of your present living situation, remarriage will change it. Most people settle in a little more when they remarry. But the settling in often causes problems, particularly for two independent persons, no matter how much they love each other. Furthermore, merging two households is a real test of your compatibility. And while it's hard enough to decide what to do with two sets of furniture, numerous personal treasures, and assorted household belongings, for many couples marrying also means finding a new place to live. And moving is always a traumatic experience. There are, however, some easy ways to go about rearranging your lives.

As a starter, plan to compromise whenever possible. *And* try to maintain your sense of humor. Admitting that this is a tension-provoking situation helps, too, for it clears the air. Remember that you chose this person because you love him and he loves you, and a few possessions that either of you hate should not be cause for great alarm. And there are worse things in life than having to put up with a few possessions that you can't stand, especially when they come along with a person you love.

Finally, even if you are one of the world's great procrastinators, try to do everything you possibly can *before* you get married. Find an apartment. Buy a house or condominium. Find new schools for the kids. Buy a new sofa and make sure it is delivered before you start living in your new home. Plan changes and arrangements down to the last detail. Make sure there are clean sheets on the beds and food in the refrigerator for everyone the first night that you spend together. It's no good starting any marriage in the midst of a totally disorganized life. And since you will quite naturally have greater trepidations about this marriage than your previous one, you especially need to get things off on an even keel.

Merging your two households won't be all agony anyway. Nest-building is, for most persons, a highly rewarding activity, and there are some special rewards that come with planning this household. For one thing, presumably you have run a household before and you know how to go about doing these things smoothly. Second, you're older and surer of yourselves. That means your taste is better developed, and while this may cause a few problems if you don't jibe with each other in all areas, you probably won't let your mother pressure you into buying china and glassware that reflect her taste instead of yours, as many brides do the first time they marry.

Finally, you won't get so many gifts this time (and you certainly can't use a bridal registry), and the ones that you do get will be tokens of affection rather than displays of value. That's bad, if you haven't completed your china and silver, but it's good if you want *this* household to reflect your taste. The people who do give you presents this time around will also be more attuned to your lifestyle, and you're more likely to get presents that you truly like and enjoy. More important, you'll do most of the buying yourselves. You can buy exactly what you want this time.

THE OFFICIAL MOVE

The etiquette of your new living arrangements is this: you can move into his home, he can move into your home, or you can both make a new home together. This applies equally to divorced persons and widowed persons. A man who has never been married before may feel comfortable moving into the home of a widow when they marry each other. A woman who is divorced may prefer to move into a man's home when she remarries. And even persons who have been living together report that the decision to marry often shakes up their lives so they often find themselves doing any of the numerous things that people do when they have decided to make their living arrangements more permanent. When deciding where to live, all you have to do is take one another's feelings into account, along with a few practical matters discussed later.

Generally, divorced persons make new homes for themselves after the divorce, but if they are living where they lived with their former spouses, this may create enough discomfort for a divorced person who is remarrying to want to find a new place to live.

DECIDING ON THE MOVE

The first thing you must discuss, then, whether you are widowed or divorced, is where you will live. In some cities with particularly tight housing markets, wedding dates are even planned around the end of leases.

If you're going to move, you also have to decide whether you want to live in an apartment or buy something. Either way, you must take into account whether children will be living with you, your personal lifestyles (Do you need lots of privacy? Does one of you have a hobby that requires space? Do you like open living?), convenience, and cost. Convenience usually means that you find a home somewhere close to where you both work and in a neighborhood that offers good shopping and transportation.

This is also a time when many persons begin to think about owning something, either a house, a condominium, or a cooperative apartment. You probably have two incomes to fall back on, or you may just resent the fact that rent money is simply gone year after year with nothing to show for it.

If you plan to buy, the first step is to decide what you can afford. Talk to your banker or financial consultant: work out a budget: decide which of your assets you will pool: and then figure out how much you can afford to spend on a place to live. Experts used to say you could afford a house valued at 2½ to 3 times your gross income, but those were the days when a woman's income was rarely taken into consideration and houses did not cost an arm and a leg. Today, a woman's income is nearly always considered, and with inflation and the soaring costs of real estate, the standard has changed somewhat. Many experts suggest that you figure out what you can afford to spend each month on rent and then multiply that amount by 100. If you can afford a $600 per month rent, then you can afford to invest $60,000 in a place to live. Alternately, you can simply sit down together and figure out what you can—and are willing to—spend each month on a mortgage and other expenses.

Once you have determined what you can afford to spend, your next concern will be *where* you can afford it. In small towns, there still exists the notion of "good" and "bad" neighborhoods. In larger communities and in cities, however, this idea has pretty much fallen by the wayside, and persons are investing quite successfully in

marginal and even bad neighborhoods with the hope
that they will catch on, thus causing real estate values to
rise and the value of their property to increase. Realtors
and financial advisors are telling young couples to buy
whatever they can afford, especially to take a chance on a
neighborhood that shows signs of improving, with the
idea that they can buy "up" again every few years, until
they get the house, co-op, or condo that they feel they
can live in for several years. The buying situation is
highly regional though (in Manhattan, Los Angeles, and
San Francisco, for example, real estate prices are very
inflated), and you should talk to bankers and realtors in
your community before you start looking. If you have
enough time, allow six months to a year to find a place to
live.

Finding a new apartment, too, can be a time-
consuming and nerve-racking chore, but if you're living
in one, you probably know how to go about getting
another one. The times when persons change apartments and the methods of finding them vary so much
from community to community that specific hints won't
be given here. Before you rent an apartment, though,
you do need to sit down and figure out what you can
afford and where you want to live.

MERGING WHAT YOU OWN

What if he has chrome and glass, and you have
collected turn-of-the-century antiques? What if he has a
collection of wood steering wheels that you hate, while
he, in turn, thinks your collection of paperweights is not
exactly something he wants in his living room? How do
you compromise? The first thing you do is find a place to

live and let the space limitations solve some of your problems. Maybe there won't be room for the steering wheels.

Since two households can't possibly fit into one, this is a time to sort out and sell or throw away a lot of things. If something really matters to you, then you should not give it up, but if you merely collected paperweights because you wanted to collect something, and you haven't looked at the collection in a year, to say nothing of adding to it, then maybe you should consider selling it. In return for which he may offer to relegate his steering wheel collection to the den or even to his office.

After you have decided which of your belongings will work with your new life, it's time to talk about the new things that you will need. If you can possibly afford to, try to start out with a few new things in your household. Since you will be doing a lot of entertaining, new dishes or flatware are nice, but you may also decide that you want a new sofa, a new bed, or new linens.

As you decide what purchases to make for your new life, remember that you don't have to pay attention to the "shoulds" anymore. You "should" not get china if you want a nice set of pottery, and if that is what will fit into your life most easily. You "should" not get silver if you don't think you will use it much.

Once you have determined to buy only what you and your future husband like, you will probably want to check popular trends in housewares and furniture, so you can blend what's new and interesting with your personal taste. Here's a brief rundown on trends to get you started. Also check out decorator's magazines and visit local department stores and furniture stores to see what's new.

Furniture. Contemporary furniture is still going strong, but its lines have become softer. Large, over-stuffed upholstered furniture is one trend these days; it runs neck and neck with a craving for high-tech. Nostalgia is strong, too, and furniture designers are preparing lines to meet what they feel will be a growing demand for Victorian and Edwardian furniture.

The interest in periods continues, which means that many persons are still decorating their homes in Early American, Art Deco, fifties furniture, and in other period styles. As antiques become dearer, collectors move up the collecting period, and there is now a renewed interest in furniture and housewares from the 1950s.

Eclecticism, or a mixture of your favorite things, is always a good way to decorate, and it is an excellent way to combine two households. You *can* put his chrome and glass tables with your old oak table, and they *will* look stunning.

CHOOSING OR ADDING TO HOUSEWARES

The next most obvious area of needs will be dishes, glassware, and flatware—everything you need to set an attractive table and entertain your friends and new family. This is also the biggest area where women are influenced by their mothers the first time around, and the area where most women would like to start all over if they could. Even if your mother didn't influence you much, *your* tastes may have changed. You may have discovered that you really don't like the elaborate china you picked and would love a new, plainer pattern, or you may have discovered that pewter is the metal that you love, and that you would be willing to unload all eight of your sterling place settings for the equivalent in pewter. Now is the time to think about doing these things. You're starting a new life with a new person— and you may never have so much of an opportunity to start all over again.

Housewares have become much more casual in design and style in recent years. Many women, especially those who work, are finding that they prefer to use stoneware or pottery, something they can dress up when they want to and still use when the family is eating alone. On the other hand, china shows up more and more for everyday meals, as women realize that they don't have to use it only on once-a-year special occasions.

Dishes

When buying dishes, you need to think about style, color, formality, price, and open stock. The latter, which means that the dishes will be available by the piece for some time to come, is especially important if you are not buying a full set of dishes all at once, or if you are planning to add only a few dishes to your present set. While styles in dishes have shifted from the use of china to stoneware, it is interesting to note that the all-time, best-selling dish patterns have not changed much over the years. "Drabware" by Wedgewood, a plain yet highly versatile and interesting pattern that was reintroduced a few years ago, is the all-time, best-selling pattern at Tiffany's. But the best-selling pattern of all time, a hit since it was introduced in the forties, is Franciscan's "Desert Rose." It is selling stronger than ever today, perhaps because its timeless pink-and-green flowered pattern goes hand in hand with the return to romanticism in table linens and home decorating in general.

Whether you are selecting new dishes or filling in your old set, you may need additional dishes to meet the needs of your new family. You should have enough dishes to get you through the day, and enough to serve six to eight persons for a company dinner, without scurrying out to the kitchen to wash the dishes for the next course.

Whereas most first-time brides choose a fine china and an everyday china, you may well find that your needs are quite different. If you work, you probably won't even consider serving a four-course evening meal on good china, and if you are becoming the mother of a couple of rambunctious children, you would also be wise not to push the use of your good china for dinner. Instead, consider one of the alternatives, which are described here:

Earthenware, thicker and heavier than china, is also soft, which makes it susceptible to chips and breaks. It's probably not a good choice if you have young children around, but is a good informal dishware for everyday use otherwise. A lot of interesting, casual patterns are available.

Stoneware, extremely hard and dense, is a good dish for everyday use. It is opaque and heavy. Stoneware comes in a variety of qualities and corresponding prices. Stoneware, which used to be reserved for teapots and heavy serving dishes, is available in everyday sets of dishes today.

Ironstone is a kind of earthenware that is often done in plain white, with a glazed finish. Since white dishes are so versatile, you may want to look into a set of ironstone, particularly if you have a lot of printed or striped table linens. Ironstone is often found in nice, inexpensive sets. It's very sturdy.

Oven-to-tableware, the newest development in dishes, is made of many different types of clay. It is backed by a manufacturer's guarantee that within a specified number of years, it will not break, chip, crack, or develop fine lines in the glaze due to the heat. It has recently come out in some trendy new designs that you won't be at all embarrassed to put on your table even for company, and it's particularly practical for anyone who leads a busy life—such as a working wife and mother.

Melamine, a practical, break-resistant plastic, isn't the kind of thing that generates romance at quiet little dinners *à deux*, nor will you want to serve company on it, *but* it may be perfect for your ready-made family, especially if you think you are going to be sensitive to such things as the sound of your china breaking.

Eight five-piece place settings is usually adequate, unless your family is bigger, in which case you need at least one place setting per person. The traditional five-piece place setting consists of a dinner plate, a salad plate, a soup or dessert bowl, and a cup and saucer. From entertaining over the years, you may know that this place setting doesn't work for you and you may want a bread and butter plate, which can also double as a dessert plate, instead of a soup bowl, for example. You will probably be charged for the difference, but the cost won't be more than a few dollars, and it is worth it to have the dishes that work best for the kind of meals you serve. Even if you do buy the standard five-piece place setting, the next thing you will probably want to add to it is the bread and butter plate; it's versatile and can be used for a dessert, bread, or a first course plate. If you are buying stoneware or even some inexpensive kinds of china, you may be able to find a special price for a 20-piece starter set, or you may want a 45- or 53-piece starter set, which consists of eight five-piece place settings, plus a vegetable bowl, a serving plate, and a sugar and creamer.

Flatware

Since sterling has become so expensive, many women are choosing instead to buy quality stainless or silverplate or any of the new, interesting metal alloys that have been developed recently. Even if you do buy silver, try to buy something you can use every day. Silver does not need to be cleaned more than twice a year if you use it regularly, and regular use helps to build up a patina, that soft, glowing finish silver acquires with use and age. These days, most couples are choosing fairly plain silver patterns that can be used with either fine china or everyday dishes. Tiffany's "Faneuil" is a leading seller in that store, and Gorham's "Chantilly," first introduced in 1895, has been a favorite choice since it was first issued.

There is a plethora of flatware from which to choose today, and there is no reason not to set your table with any of the interesting alternates to sterling. Whatever you buy, when you are talking with the salesperson, be sure to ask exactly what you are looking at. Also ask about its maintenance, wearing qualities, and whether or not it is dishwasher proof.

To refresh your memory and perhaps introduce you to some new ideas in flatware:

Sterling flatware is 925 per 1000 parts pure silver. Pure silver is too soft to craft into flatware, so a small amount of another metal is alloyed with the silver. "Sterling" is stamped somewhere on each piece of sterling, and you should look for its mark before you buy anything advertised as sterling. Sometimes, to reduce the cost, a hollow handle is used in the knives.

Silverplate, which has gained tremendously in popularity in recent years, is pure silver electroplated onto another metal. If the silverplate is heavy, it will last for many years. The quality varies with the manufacturer, and you should buy from a reputable dealer or department store, and talk with the salesperson about the varying levels of quality. Also, by looking at enough silverplate, you will soon develop an eye for what is good and what isn't.

Vermeil is silver flatware electroplated with gold; it is the most expensive flatware you can buy. Vermeil comes in a wide range of styles.

Stainless steel, which used to be considered suitable

only for everyday use, has moved into the realm of company use. It is made of nonprecious metal. It comes in several finishes: satin, pewter, and mirror. Satin, the best-selling type of stainless, has a slightly dulled finish. Pewter, as you might guess, looks like pewter, and a mirror finish is shiny.

Quality is important in stainless, particularly if you are going to use it every day for several years. Be sure you buy 18/8 or 18/10 chrome/nickel steel. Check the weight by holding it; after you have held several varieties of stainless, you will develop a feel for a good solid one. Also check the balance; this is important with any eating utensil.

Pewter, a tin alloy, has made a deserved comeback in recent years and is worth looking into for its beauty and its lasting qualities, and because it is, so far, less expensive than sterling. Pewter comes in an antique or a polished finish. The polished finish acquires the same patina as sterling.

There are two other possibilities in flatware: *pewterware* and *Sterling II*. Pewterware is a flatware electroplated with pewter, and Sterling II is a combination of stainless steel tines, cutting blades, and spoon bowls with hollow, sterling handles. Both are available in many interesting patterns and are especially worth looking into if money is a factor.

You will probably need at least eight settings of flatware to entertain with ease, and you should have one place setting for every member of your family. A four-piece place setting of flatware includes a meat knife, dinner fork, salad fork, and teaspoon.

Crystal and Glassware

The major trend in wine glasses is toward an all-purpose, clear, large goblet. Serious drinkers insist that a wine glass must be clear so they can appreciate the beauty of the wine's color, and you need a glass large enough to let wines breathe. But another trend—undoubtedly part of the interest in romanticism—is toward colored wine glasses. Thirty percent of all wine glasses now sold are made of colored glass. You will need enough wine glasses to serve eight to ten persons for dinner. You can base the number of wine glasses you need on the number you can serve at dinner.

It's also nice to have sherry glasses and some brandy snifters, as well as a good supply of glasses for mixed drinks. Then there are everyday glasses—what you use for drinking water, pouring soft drinks, and glasses of milk. Especially if you will be adding children to your household, you will need an endless supply of glasses, preferably of the unbreakable, inexpensive type. Your best bet, if you can't buy directly from the manufacturer, is to find a discount housewares store that will supply your continuing needs.

Linens

Prints and pretty colors are increasingly popular, since entertaining has become more informal. Traditional white tablecloths, place mats, and napkins are always correct, though. Wildflower patterns are enjoying immense popularity right now, and colored sheets continue to sell well, although there has been a slight trend back to white sheets.

Your major problem in linens will probably be fitting in what you already own with what you need for your new life and for your new expanded family. Try to build a wardrobe of linens, in other words, buy things that go with each other. If you own a lot of print table-cloths and place mats, and you need to replace some napkins that have worn out over the years, then think in terms of buying one or two sets of contrasting solid-colored napkins rather than trying to match them to tablecloths and place mats you already own.

The hardest linens to coordinate in a new home are those for the bathroom, especially if you already own towels that don't match the new bathroom. Some women always want towels that match their bathroom colors, and others, more aware of how mobile most person's lives have become, settle on towels in good basic colors that will, with any luck, go with almost anything. One helpful hint is to buy equal quantities of light and dark towels to balance out the laundry loads.

If your family will grow with the sudden addition of children, you will undoubtedly need to buy more towels than you now have, especially if you have been living alone. It is almost impossible to say how many sets you will need per person, but with children, you probably should have three or four sets of towels per person just to cover emergencies and guests.

Towels come in several textures: sheared terry, which is velvety to the touch and not very absorbent; plain terry; jacquard, which is a combination of sheared and unsheared terry; and linen, which is mostly used for dish towels and hand towels for guests. Deciding on the kind and color of towels and other bathroom linens is a matter of personal taste, but the choices are wide these days as more and more designers are adding their signatures to new, varied lines.

Many brides who are remarrying indulge in the luxury of new bed linens. With the great variety today, there is no reason not to find exactly what you like. There are solid bright colors and solid pastels, sheets with lace trims and sheets with interesting borders in a great variety of designs. You can create any mood you want in your bedroom mostly through your choice of sheets. The best sheets that you can buy are cotton percale, although the new 50/50 cotton polyesters require little upkeep and are very nice to the touch. Muslin is not as soft as the other two materials, but it is suitable if that is what you can afford.

Cookware

The two lists that follow, one for household general needs and the other for kitchen needs, should help you plan and also help you spot any items you may need to make your new household run as smoothly as possible.

NECESSARY

- [ ] 2 saucepans: 1-quart, 2½-quart
- [ ] 2 skillets: 8-inch, 10-inch
- [ ] Double boiler
- [ ] Kettle
- [ ] Dutch oven
- [ ] Roasting pan with rack
- [ ] 2-quart round casserole
- [ ] 2-quart rectangular baking dish
- [ ] 2 cake pans: 9-inch rounds
- [ ] Cookie sheets
- [ ] 2 loaf pans
- [ ] Pie plate
- [ ] Set of mixing bowls
- [ ] Wooden spoons

- [ ] Utensil set (ladle, masher, etc.)
- [ ] Wire whisk
- [ ] Rotary egg beater
- [ ] Measuring cups and spoons
- [ ] Salad bowl and servers
- [ ] Knives, for carving and cutting
- [ ] Knife sharpener
- [ ] Wooden cutting board
- [ ] Grater
- [ ] Colander and strainer
- [ ] Metal tongs
- [ ] Corkscrew
- [ ] Can and bottle opener
- [ ] Vegetable peeler
- [ ] Reamer (citrus juicer)
- [ ] Salt and pepper mills
- [ ] Kitchen shears
- [ ] Coffeemaker
- [ ] 60-minute timer
- [ ] Plastic storage containers
- [ ] Ice trays
- [ ] Vegetable and dish scrubbers
- [ ] Dish towels
- [ ] Potholders
- [ ] Dish drainer
- [ ] Wastebasket
- [ ] Rubber bowl scrapers

NEXT IN IMPORTANCE

- [ ] Spice rack
- [ ] Vegetable steamer
- [ ] Blender
- [ ] Toaster or toaster oven
- [ ] Electric mixer with dough hook
- [ ] Rolling pin
- [ ] Pastry brush

- [ ] Pastry blender
- [ ] Flour sifter
- [ ] Muffin tin
- [ ] Spring form, removable bottom
- [ ] Tube (angel food cake) pan
- [ ] Soufflé dish
- [ ] Quiche plate
- [ ] Molds, different sizes
- [ ] Custard cups or ramekins
- [ ] Poached egg pan
- [ ] Oven thermometer
- [ ] Meat thermometer
- [ ] Boning knife
- [ ] Carving fork
- [ ] Knife rack or holster
- [ ] Garlic press
- [ ] Egg slicer
- [ ] Salad spinner
- [ ] Apple corer
- [ ] Bulb baster
- [ ] Barbecue skewers

NICE EXTRAS

- [ ] Food processor
- [ ] Microwave oven
- [ ] Slow cooker
- [ ] Coffee grinder
- [ ] Juice extractor
- [ ] Pressure cooker
- [ ] Deep fryer
- [ ] Waffle iron
- [ ] Ice-cream maker
- [ ] Wok
- [ ] Funnels
- [ ] Kitchen scale
- [ ] Marble pastry slab

☐ Hot tray
☐ Clay cooker
☐ Fish poacher
☐ Melon ball scoop
☐ Ice-cream scoop
☐ Biscuit and cookie cutters
☐ Pastry bag and attachments
☐ Trussing needle, lacing pins
☐ Cookbook holder

BASIC HOUSEWARES CHECKLIST

Fine Flatware		Quantity	
		Have	Need
Number of place settings		____	____
Spoons	Tea	____	____
	Soup/Dessert	____	____
	Table	____	____
	Demitasse	____	____
	Iced tea	____	____
Forks	Dinner	____	____
	Dessert/Salad	____	____
Knives	Dinner	____	____
	Butter spreader	____	____
	Steak	____	____
Serving	Butter knife	____	____
	Cold meat fork	____	____
	Lemon fork	____	____
	Pie server	____	____
	Cake knife	____	____
	Sugar spoon	____	____
	Gravy ladle	____	____
	Serving forks	____	____
	Serving spoons	____	____
	Roast set	____	____
	Steak set	____	____
	Salad set	____	____

		Quantity	
Everyday Flatware		Have	Need
Number of place settings		____	____
Hollow ware	Tea service	____	____
	Coffee service	____	____
	Serving trays	____	____
	Platters	____	____
	Vegetable dishes	____	____
	Bread tray	____	____
	Gravy boat	____	____
	Sauce bowl	____	____
	Salt/Pepper set	____	____
	Sugar/Creamer	____	____
	Water pitcher	____	____
	Candlesticks	____	____
China			
Number of place settings		____	____
Plates	Luncheon/Salad	____	____
	Dinner	____	____
	Dessert	____	____
	Bread and butter	____	____
Dishes	Soup	____	____
	Fruit/Cereal	____	____
Cups	Tea and saucer	____	____
	Coffee and saucer	____	____
	Demitasse and saucer	____	____
Serving	Vegetable dishes	____	____
	Gravy boat	____	____
	Sugar/Creamer	____	____
	Platters	____	____
	Bowls	____	____
	Coffee pot	____	____
	Tea pot	____	____
Everyday Dinnerware			
Number of place settings		____	____

	Quantity	
	Have	*Need*

Fine Glassware

Number of place settings   ____   ____
            Goblets   ____   ____
            Wine   ____   ____
            Champagne/Sherbet ____   ____
            Cocktail   ____   ____
            Liqueur   ____   ____

Everyday Glassware

Number of place settings   ____   ____
            Water glasses   ____   ____
            Fruit juice   ____   ____
            Highball   ____   ____
            Old-fashioned   ____   ____
            Brandy   ____   ____
            Iced tea   ____   ____
            Beer   ____   ____
            Dessert dishes   ____   ____
            Plates   ____   ____
            Bowls   ____   ____
            Water pitcher   ____   ____
            Sugar/Creamer   ____   ____
            Condiment dishes ____   ____
            Compote   ____   ____
            Candlestick   ____   ____
            Salt/Pepper set   ____   ____

Linens

Dining Room Formal dinner
            cloths/napkins   ____   ____
           Informal
            cloths/napkins   ____   ____
           Placemat sets   ____   ____
           Cocktail napkins   ____   ____
Bathroom   Bath towels   ____   ____

		Quantity	
		Have	Need
	Hand towels	———	———
	Bath sheets	———	———
	Fingertip towels	———	———
	Washcloths	———	———
	Bath mats	———	———
	Rug/Lid cover set	———	———
	Shower curtain	———	———
Bedroom	Sheets	———	———
	Cases	———	———
	Pillows	———	———
	Blankets	———	———
	Comforter	———	———
	Bedspread	———	———
Kitchen	Dish towels	———	———
	Pot holders	———	———

Housewares

	Vacuum cleaner/ Electric broom	———	———
	Dustpan/Brush	———	———
	Broom	———	———
	Mop	———	———
	Ironing board	———	———
	Iron	———	———
	Laundry hamper	———	———
	Garbage pail	———	———
	Step stool	———	———
	Tool kit	———	———

Furniture

Living Room	Sofa/Sofa bed	———	———
	Chairs	———	———
	Coffee table	———	———
	End tables	———	———
	Lamps	———	———

		Quantity	
---	---	Have	Need
	Shelves	_____	_____
	Curtains	_____	_____
	Draperies	_____	_____
Bedroom	Bed	_____	_____
	Mattress/Springs	_____	_____
	Night table	_____	_____
	Chest/Armoire	_____	_____
	Lamps	_____	_____
	Curtains	_____	_____
	Draperies	_____	_____
Dining Room	Table	_____	_____
	Chairs	_____	_____
	Buffet/Storage	_____	_____
	Curtains	_____	_____
	Draperies	_____	_____

Creature Comforts

	Rugs	_____	_____
	Clocks	_____	_____
	Mirrors	_____	_____
	Tray tables	_____	_____
	Television	_____	_____
	Sound system	_____	_____
	Sewing machine	_____	_____
	Desk	_____	_____
	Bathroom scale	_____	_____

TALKING ABOUT OWNERSHIP

Talking about ownership at a time when you are starting over, one hopes, with the notion that this marriage will be forever, is not an easy thing to do, but *it is* a necessary and realistic thing to do. There are actually several reasons to discuss who owns what when you are remarrying. Odd as it may seem, it may put your minds at ease. After all, if you have been divorced you have been through this once, and things did not work out—and you did have to split up your belongings. Just acknowledging that it could happen again may ease a lot of the nervous tension you feel over marrying again.

Another reason to talk about ownership is that you own more things. You may own eight place settings of sterling that your parents gave you as a first wedding gift, or you may have bought it yourself. Either way, it is yours, and there is no reason that you should feel otherwise. While you will almost certainly want to make joint purchases as a married couple, and you probably won't feel the need to define the ownership of each item you purchase after you are married as many cohabiting couples do, you should still sit down before you marry and talk about your present possessions, possibly even draw up a contract or a written list.

The final reason that you should discuss ownership now, before you are married, is that this is the best time to do it. Remember what it was like to split possessions during your divorce, when everything had already fallen apart? That's when it is hard to sit down and talk to each other calmly and logically. And while now may not seem like the perfect romantic moment to acknowledge that things just may not work out, now is, in fact, the best time to make these decisions.

THINKING ABOUT CONTRACTS

Marriage contracts, while actually a very old idea, are being used by more and more couples these days. Some contracts are nothing more than oral, informal agreements—you do the laundry, he'll do the dishes and cooking. Other contracts are more detailed, and spell out in writing who gets what if you split, who owes whom money, and other such aspects of living together. While drawing up a written contract may seem even more appalling than deciding who owns what informally, such contracts are something to think about. They do help to eliminate unpleasantness if you happen to split up, and with more women working—and bringing home ever more substantial amounts of money—they are becoming increasingly important.

What goes in a marriage contract? You can put anything in a contract that you want to, as long as it is not illegal. Some marriage contracts limit the amount that one partner can sue another for during a divorce; others specify ownership of various properties; still others delineate provisions for support if there is a separation.

You can always draw up contracts yourselves and have them notarized, but even better is to contact a marriage and family lawyer who will help you draw them up legally.

Some persons protest that marriage contracts are cold and unfeeling, and you may well be among those persons. Even if you are, they are still worth considering and discussing. Even if you decide that marriage contracts are not good for your marriage, discussion of them and of your individual rights will clear the air, and most persons who are remarrying need to do just that.

GETTING READY TO MOVE

Once you have found the perfect home and divided up your possessions *and* made plans, if not purchases, for your new possessions, you must still organize and carry out the actual move. Although most persons have experience in moving, here is a list of the things you have to do to make the move go smoothly:

As soon as you know you are moving:
- [ ] Contact movers for estimates and settle on mover right away
- [ ] Contact local schools if move is during school year to make arrangements for children
- [ ] Arrange for storage of any furniture or other possessions
- [ ] Start changing your address on charges, magazines, and other mail

Two weeks before:
- [ ] Start packing
- [ ] Contact electric, phone, and gas companies to disconnect old accounts and establish new ones

One to two days before:
- [ ] Buy supplies you will need in new home and take them over or carry them with you when you move (if you are moving far away, you should buy supplies when you get there). These include cleaning supplies, emergency food supplies, and paper plates and utensils for the first few days. Also buy soap, toilet paper, and lots of paper towels.
- [ ] Clean your old apartment; clean your new home or make provisions for someone else to do so if it needs it.
- [ ] Make sure utilities are turned off as scheduled in your old home and are turned on in your new home.
- [ ] Pack an overnight bag to take with you and tide you over during the first few days.

You and your fiance can mostly split the moving chores between you and carry them out with little discussion. The only detail that will require a conference is the telephone. Here are some hints on ordering telephones:

1. Decide on the listing you want in the phone book, if any. Most telephone companies are aware that two persons live and work in many marriages today, and they may be willing to give you a multiple listing if you want one. Be ready to pay a small one-time fee or monthly charge if this is required to get the listing you want.

2. Most phone companies have a selection of unit-call plans. Sit down and talk over your telephone habits—how much you use the phone, for how long, and at what time of day. Also discuss where you want to use the phones. Do you have to have an extension in the kitchen? Do you feel that you are safer with a phone beside your bed? Do you want one line or two? Talk about the style of phones that you want. Does he hate the small phones that have push buttons? Do you love them? After you've talked about your needs, figure out what call package and which phones will work for you. Call the phone company back and order what you need.

3. Check your new apartment to see if there are phone jacks installed already; if so, you may be able to save some money by moving your old phones with you.

4. Place your telephone order early so the phones will be in your new home when you move in.

One key to an organized move—although it goes against most person's natural inclinations—is to make out a schedule and then follow it. No matter how painful, do everything as soon as possible and you'll eliminate a lot of pain at the end of the move when tensions are running especially high.

THE TOUCHIEST QUESTION OF ALL:
OLD WEDDING GIFTS

Never do old wedding gifts (silver bowls and trays and things like that) become more obvious than when you are beginning a new life. And while you may have worked out perfectly what furniture you will use, there may be a few tense moments the first few weeks of your new marriage when you prepare a romantic dinner using china from your first marriage or when you learn that the ashtray he dotes on was a gift from his ex-wife. Even cohabitation rarely makes these matters assume the importance that they do when you have taken the big, final step of getting married.

If you find that you are annoyed at being confronted with a daily reminder of a past marriage, speak up. Your spouse may not realize that something offends you if you don't say something directly to him about it. And listen carefully if he doesn't like something from your first marriage. If the item is replaceable—an ashtray, for example—replace it. And if it isn't, perhaps you could relegate it to storage until the day when you can afford a replacement.

If your china and silver were presents from your first marriage, you will probably not feel like storing them, nor would this be practical, but it is tactful not to eat on them for awhile—and it's a good reason to buy new everyday dishes and bed linens and other household items, if you can possibly afford to do so. You need not buy everything new; just get enough to feel that you are truly starting over—which you are.

GIVING YOURSELVES A REWARD

Undoubtedly, the hardest part of remarrying is

working out your living arrangements. And everyone should have a reward for such efforts. And since you won't be getting a lot of large wedding presents this time, why not plan to buy something really special for yourselves? Here is a list of suggestions:

silver candlesticks
set of copper pans
food processor
silver plates
soup tureen
chafing dish
crystal hurricane lamps
crystal bowl or vase
serving dishes
crystal wine, sherry, or brandy glasses
wine rack or wine storage unit
sterling serving pieces
interesting antique serving pieces—a cake platter, for example

One couple who shared a mutual interest in art and architecture treated themselves to an original Eames chair as a wedding gift. You are limited only by your imagination.

Chapter Ten

DOING IT YOUR WAY
Questions Most Frequently Asked About Remarrying

Getting married again raises lots of questions for everyone involved. Some brides want to go strictly by the book. They want everything to be done just right, perhaps so that Great Aunt Minnie who disapproved of the divorce can smilingly approve of this wedding. This bride has a special set of questions, which usually centers around the things she shouldn't do for this wedding: Is a white dress in bad taste? Can she throw her garter, or shouldn't she even be worrying about such things? Must she be married in a small, quiet ceremony with only family present?

Other brides, those who feel they missed out on something by not having a large, formal wedding the first time they married, come up with an entirely different set of questions: Can they have a large, formal wedding? Can they wear a veil? Can their children stand up for them? Can their fathers give them away?

Wherever I travel, when I talk to brides, the same questions come up over and over again about remarrying. The answers are not always clearcut. A bride who wants to follow the strictest rulebook and comes from a family that is concerned with protocol should know that a white dress and veil will be frowned upon at a second wedding. A bride whose tastes are less formal should be told that she can wear just about anything she chooses to wear, particularly if most of the guests will be her close friends. Mostly, I offer this advice to prospective brides: Do what makes you feel comfortable and what you feel like doing to make your wedding day the special occasion it should be. The persons who love you will understand if you want to depart a little bit from the accepted rulebook. For those who want more definite answers, though, here are the questions I'm most frequently asked, as well as some answers to questions about particularly tricky problems.

EXPENSES

Who pays for this wedding?
Most often, the bride and groom share expenses. You cannot expect your parents to pay for a second wedding, and his parents have no obligation to pay. If your parents do offer to pay for all or part of the wedding, there is no reason that you cannot accept. On the other hand, wouldn't it be more fun to make this wedding your own show?

How can my groom and I divide expenses? I thought he

only had to pay for the flowers, rings and his clothes? The flowers, rings, and clothes are his expenses at the first wedding where, presumably, your parents are paying for everything else. This time, if you are sharing expenses, you should split them fifty-fifty. Some brides and grooms set up a special wedding account once they have estimated what they can and what they will probably have to spend. Each takes money out to pay for whatever expenses or arrangements he or she is handling. Others just divide the money more informally as they make their plans—he may buy the liquor while you pay for the caterer. To be completely objective and fair, keep track of receipts and split all expenses.

My fiance and I have invited our honor attendants and two other couples to celebrate our wedding at our favorite French restaurant, which is very expensive. We expected to pay, but now they are insisting that they want to treat us? What should we do? If you know that treating you will not impose any hardship on any of the persons involved, then this would be a nice wedding gift from your friends.

WEDDING AND RECEPTION

My clergyman at the church I attended throughout my childhood says he cannot marry me because I am divorced. What other kind of wedding can I have? You can have a civil ceremony at city hall or be married in a judge's chambers. If you do this, I suggest that you plan a special party for your reception so that your wedding will be properly celebrated. Alternately, you can look for another minister or rabbi to marry you.

How do I go about finding another clergyman to marry me? I don't attend church anywhere, and I thought the clergyman had to know the persons he was marrying. Today, since so many persons have moved away from the communities where they were brought up, there is less of a problem than there used to be in "finding" a clergyman to marry you. Start by asking a friend whose religion is the same as yours and who was married recently. Call your neighborhood churches or a church council and ask if they can recommend a clergyman.

I just got married in Chicago, where my new husband and I have lived for several years. When we visit my parents this summer, they want to give us a wedding reception. I feel this would not be right since I was married before and since we weren't married in my hometown. It is perfectly all right for your parents to give you a reception to celebrate your marriage when you visit them this summer. It should, however, just be a reception, not a wedding reception, per se. You should buy a very pretty, nonbridish looking dress that you would wear to any party given in your honor.

Someone said I shouldn't carry a traditional bridal bouquet since I have been married before. Is this correct? By traditional bridal bouquet, I assume that you mean a cascade or some other, similar arrangement usually carried by brides. Of course you may carry one, if you want to, but don't forget the other possibilities: a basket of flowers, a nosegay, flowers pinned to your dress or worn in your hair. One lovely bride who chose a dress with streamers had small rosebuds attached to the ends of the streamers, a most unusual and pretty touch.

Can I wear a veil if I have been married before? I did not have a wedding dress or veil for my first wedding. Since a veil is a symbol of purity, it is considered more tasteful for a woman who was previously married not to wear a veil when she remarries. Whether or not you wore one the first time doesn't matter. What matters is that you were married before. You can, however, look radiant in a large, floppy hat with veiling attached or you might select one of the small cocktail hats with a small veil that covers your face. If you really want a veil, you can even have a floral headpiece made up and wear a short (no longer than your shoulders) veil that coordinates with the hat and with your dress. Avoid wearing a long veil attached to a traditional bridal headpiece.

I am about to be the mother of the bride again. The wedding is at 6 P.M., and a large reception will follow. Must I wear a mother-of-the-bride dress or can I wear a regular evening gown? Must I wear a hat to church? Even mothers of first-time brides are not wearing mother-of-the-bride dresses so often these days, and you can certainly wear your loveliest evening gown. You need not wear a hat to church, unless the church requires it. If your dress is lowcut, wear a wrap of some kind for the church ceremony. If possible, do not wear black—it's not considered festive enough for a wedding.

INVITATIONS

I still use the married name from my first marriage. I suppose this is awkward, but I have built a professional reputation with this name, and I'm not anxious to change. Any suggestions? From my mail, this situation would appear to be fairly common. The first thing you should do is ask your fiance how he feels about your name. If he objects, you might use your first name and his last name socially and keep your professional name. Many women, however, who took their first husband's names now object to using another man's name. If this is your feeling, you should keep the name you have been using— many persons will assume it is your married name anyway.

Legally, must I use my husband's surname after we are married? The laws vary from state to state, and in most states, they have become less rigid in recent years. Only one state, Hawaii, ever stated clearly that a woman legally had to use her husband's name, although other states had the means of making one do so. In Illinois, until recently, a woman had to use her married name to vote. Check with the regulations in your state—usually, you can use whatever name you want to use as long as you have no intention to defraud anyone. And you can always file for a name change—back to the name you want to use if marriage has legally changed your name.

I am getting married Wednesday in a private ceremony and the following Saturday my new husband and I are inviting our friends to a wedding reception. I'm also planning to use my new husband's surname, and that is my problem. We are unsure how the invitations–which we are issuing–should read. Do not use your new name on the invitations, since this could be confusing to some friends and acquaintances who may not be able to identify you with your new name. If several weeks were elapsing between your wedding and the reception, then you would use your new married name. But with such a short amount of time you should issue invitations that read as follows:

> *The pleasure of your company*
> *is requested at the wedding reception of*
> *Miss Pamela Jones*
> [*or Mrs. Pamela Jones or Mrs. Hanson Jones,*
> *if Jones is your ex-husband's name*]
> *and*
> *Mr. George Henderson*
> etc.

I am planning a small second wedding. I'm calling my friends and close family to invite them personally. My mother insists on sending engraved announcements. I say this is improper. Who is right? Your mother is. Engraved announcements can properly be sent after any size wedding regardless of how many times you have been married. Their only purpose is to inform friends that you have married.

CHILDREN

My two sons, ages eight and ten, want to stand up with me during the ceremony? I've never heard of a bride being attended by two little boys. What can I do? Let your sons stand proudly beside you and be happy that they are supportive of you in your new life. Weddings are much less formal these days, and at second weddings in particular, persons expect children to be accommodated. I have one suggestion: when you and your new husband walk back up the aisle, your children might join their grandparents or some other close relative and then leave the church with them.

I am a fifty-four-year-old divorcee who is marrying a man ten years my senior. My eldest son feels it is his place to give me away. What is the etiquette on this? Divorced women of any age are not given in marriage—in fact, a woman is given in marriage only once, and these days, that is too much for some women. Nix that idea, but depending upon your son's age, see if you can't think of some other way for him to participate. Perhaps he could greet and seat the guests as they arrive?

My fifteen-year-old daughter is going to be my attendant at my wedding. She is very excited about being a bridesmaid and wants a traditional bridesmaid dress. Is this okay? This depends upon the degree of formality and what you are wearing; if you wear street clothes, she should wear them. If you are wearing a long dress, she could have one, but she might be more suitably dressed in a party dress designed for her age than in a bridesmaid dress.

REMARRYING A FORMER SPOUSE

I am remarrying a man to whom I was married for ten years. We have been divorced for three years. What kind of ceremony is best? A small quiet ceremony is most appropriate for you. You can be married in a civil ceremony or in a church.

BLESSING OF A MARRIAGE

I have made plans to be married in a civil ceremony–too many plans to cancel now, but I am feeling that I would rather have some sort of religious ceremony. What can I do? Go ahead with the civil ceremony, but then arrange for a church blessing. Many religions have a blessing ceremony for persons who have been married earlier in civil ceremonies, and if your church doesn't, maybe the clergyman would help you write one.

FORMER INLAWS AS WEDDING GUESTS

Which, if any, of my former inlaws must I invite to my wedding? You may invite any ex-inlaws that you and your fiance feel comfortable with—and you are under no obligation to ask any of them, even if you have remained good friends. They'll understand if their presence would make you feel uncomfortable.

I am very good friends with my ex-brother-in-law, but he was the best man at my first wedding, and I don't feel like inviting him to this one. How can I tell him this? Are you having a small, private ceremony? If so, you need not explain to anyone why you have not invited them except to say that you are having only a few relatives. If you are having many guests at the ceremony, then you probably should discuss this with him. He may not feel like coming, or he may be hurt if he doesn't attend—either way, though, he will probably respect your feelings and not let this ruin a longstanding friendship.

PRESENTS

I'm getting married for the third time. When I got married the second time, many of my friends gave me wedding gifts, and I feel bad to think that they might give me gifts again. Can I write "no gifts, please" on the invitations? No, you can't. That's almost as bad as writing "bring gifts, please." No one is obligated to buy you a wedding gift if they gave you one for your first wedding. Your close friends will probably want to give you something for your new home—and others simply won't feel obligated. Don't worry about it.

I was married only briefly several years ago in another community. I'm getting married again, and am planning a sizeable wedding and reception. Can I register for gifts at the department store in my town? I'm sorry, but you can't. That's a prerogative of first-time brides only, and it would be in bad taste for you to register for gifts for this wedding.

My second marriage lasted only two months. Must I return the wedding presents I was given? No, you need not return the gifts. You should offer to return any of the groom's family heirlooms that you may have been given, and he should be permitted to pick any wedding gifts that may have special meaning to him. If a marriage is annulled shortly after it occurs or if it is called off at the last minute, then wedding gifts should be returned.

What kind of gift is appropriate for a second wedding when the bride has been living in her own household for several years? For one thing, you can buy a less expensive wedding gift if you want to, and it need not be something of lasting value, as it would be for a first wedding. Generally, traditional "wedding" gifts— blankets, toasters, and silver—are not given. Think about giving a bottle of rare wine to a newly married couple. Or you might treat them to dinner one night (in absentia, of course) on their wedding trip. If they live in a city, they might appreciate season tickets to ballet, symphony, or theater. Think about their special interests—and buy them something to accommodate them.

I eloped the first time I married, so I'm having a large formal wedding this time. Can I or am I expected to display my wedding gifts? No, you shouldn't officially display your wedding gifts because no one is obligated to give you presents this time. Along the same line, if persons bring gifts to the wedding, you shouldn't open them there in front of guests who may not have brought you a gift.

SPECIAL CIRCUMSTANCES

I am getting married for the third time. I know it is inappropriate for me to have a very large, ceremonious wedding, but is there anything I can't do because this is my third wedding? Obviously, you should keep the wedding small and intimate, but there are no special rules that apply to this wedding other than the ones suggested throughout the book.

I am a widow, technically, of only a few months. My husband was missing in action and presumed dead for five years before I learned "officially" of his death. Must I post-pone my wedding because I have recently received news of my first husband's death? No, you have mourned and suffered enough. Continue with your wedding plans.

I am supposed to be married in two weeks and have been planning the wedding for eight months. I recently learned that my ex-husband is dying. Our two children are, of course, very upset. Should I postpone my wedding? No rules of etiquette cover such a situation—you must simply weigh the feelings of all involved. Your children's lives are obviously very upset right now, and you may find it impossible to cope with starting married life and them at the same time. Then, too, their father may die or take a turn for the worse the week of your wedding, causing a last-minute postponement anyway. Possibly you should consider scaling down your wedding or making contingency plans in the event that the worst does happen.

I am a divorcee with two young children who is plan-ning to marry again. I have always worn my elaborately jeweled wedding ring from my first wedding, mostly for the children's sakes. The ring is very valuable, and I'm not sure what to do with it. It's time to put that ring away. Tuck it away and save it to give to one of your children when he or she is older. Alternately, you could have the stones reset into a piece of jewelry you could wear now.

I am planning to marry again. I have a two-year-old daughter. Needless to say, she requires a lot of attention, and I'm not particularly interested in having her present at the wedding for this reason. Lots of persons, though, have asked whether or not she should be there, and I'm beginning to think she should be present. What do you think? Never mind what others think and leave her at home. This is your special day, after all, and besides, she can't dance yet, can she?

INDEX

217

name changes and, 21-23,
    208-9
to the reception, 31-33, 37-38
by telephone, 29, 209
wording of formal, 31-38
Ironstone dishes, 183

Jewelry, 59
Jewish weddings, 72, 73, 98

Kissing the bride, 106

Linens, 187-89
Lingerie, 57
Luncheons, 137-38

Maps, 42
Marriage contracts, 197-98
Marriage license, 86
Melamine dishes, 183
Menu cards, 95-96
Menus:
    for breakfasts, luncheons, and
        brunches, 137-38
    for formal sit-down dinners,
        144-45
    for restaurant reception, 152
    for sit-down buffets, 140-41
    for stand-up buffets, 135-36
    for supper dances, 146-47
    tea, 130-31
    themes for, 147-49
Money, 6-7, 160-62, 204-205
Moving to a new home, 174-76,
    198-200
    See also Housekeeping, setting
        up
Music, 12
    for church wedding, 73-74, 80,
        81, 84
    for a garden wedding, 104
    for a home wedding, 100-101,
        106
    for reception, 124

Musicians, 123-25

Name cards, 138
Name changes, 21-23, 164-65,
    208, 209
Newspaper announcements, 5

Oven-to-tableware dishes, 183
Ownership, talking about,
    196-97

Parents, 204
    divorced, 35-36, 79-80
    dress for, 68, 207
    home wedding and, 90
    reception at home of, 206
    seating of, at church wedding,
        79-80
Parties before the wedding,
    13-14, 154, 155
Party supply rental agencies,
    119-20
Past, talking about the, 158-60
Perfume, 63
Pewter flatware, 186
Pewterware flatware, 186
Photographs, 75-76, 122-23
Place cards, 153
Plane cards, 42
Plate cards, 141
Presents, see Gifts
Printed invitations, 30, 209
Private weddings, 23, 209, 211
Processional, 80-82
    at-home or garden wedding,
        106
Punches, 149-51
Purse, 58

Receiving line, 12-13
Reception, 6, 109-56, 206-207
    appropriate traditions for the,
        12-13